T0277168

Cambridge Elements ≡

Elements in Psychology and Culture
edited by
Kenneth Keith
University of San Diego

MEASURING AND INTERPRETING SUBJECTIVE WELLBEING IN DIFFERENT CULTURAL CONTEXTS

A Review and Way Forward

Robert A. Cummins
Deakin University, Victoria

CAMBRIDGE
UNIVERSITY PRESS

CAMBRIDGE
UNIVERSITY PRESS

University Printing House, Cambridge CB2 8BS, United Kingdom

One Liberty Plaza, 20th Floor, New York, NY 10006, USA

477 Williamstown Road, Port Melbourne, VIC 3207, Australia

314–321, 3rd Floor, Plot 3, Splendor Forum, Jasola District Centre,
New Delhi – 110025, India

79 Anson Road, #06–04/06, Singapore 079906

Cambridge University Press is part of the University of Cambridge.

It furthers the University's mission by disseminating knowledge in the pursuit of education, learning, and research at the highest international levels of excellence.

www.cambridge.org
Information on this title: www.cambridge.org/9781108461696
DOI: 10.1017/9781108685580

First published 2018

A catalogue record for this publication is available from the British Library.

ISBN 978-1-108-46169-6 Paperback
ISSN 2515-3986 (online)
ISSN 2515-3943 (print)

Measuring and Interpreting Subjective Wellbeing in Different Cultural Contexts

A Review and Way Forward

Robert A. Cummins

Abstract: *The scientific study of 'wellbeing' involves both objective and subjective variables. While objective wellbeing can be simply measured as tangible aspects of the living environment, measuring subjective wellbeing involves quantifying self-reported feelings. Although reliable and valid measures can be achieved, in a cross-cultural context, differences in language and culture present formidable challenges to measurement comparability. This Element begins by describing the behaviour of subjective wellbeing in single cultures, using the theory of homeostasis. Robert A. Cummins then discusses cross-cultural differences in subjective wellbeing, with a focus on measurement invariance as a means of ensuring the validity of comparative results. Cummins proposes that the major barrier to creating such comparability of measurement is a pervasive response bias that differs among cultures. He concludes that current instruments are inadequate to provide valid cross-cultural measures of subjective wellbeing, and that suitable measures may be created as short forms of current scales. Cummins also proposes a study design to demonstrate cultural response bias.*

Keywords: *cultural response bias, subjective wellbeing, measurement invariance, cross-cultural comparisons*

ISSNs: *2515–3986 (online), 2515–3943 (print)*

ISBNs: *9781108461696 (PB), 9781108685580 (OC)*

1 Introduction

This review concerns the overlap of two ambiguous constructs: culture and life quality. Culture can be defined using various criteria. The most widely used and enduring is Hofstede's (1984) four-dimensional typology: individualism–collectivism, power distance, masculinity, and uncertainty avoidance. However, the central issue to be discussed concerns subjective wellbeing (SWB) measurement and the tendency for cultures to differentially bias responding to personal questions. So a more useful separation of cultures for this purpose is provided by Huntington (1996). He defined the world's cultural regions by religion as Western, Orthodox, Confucian, Japanese, Latin American, Hindu, Buddhists, Islamic, African, and Sinic (pp. 45–47). The comparative cultures to be employed for this review are 'Western' and 'Confucian', even while acknowledging the very heterogeneous composition of each region.

Life quality is simpler to describe, as a universal concern among all life forms and a major driving force behind evolution. The evolutionary survival of animals and plants depends on three abilities: to acquire energy, to avoid predation, and to have progeny which then successfully reproduce. The probability for each of these conditions being met reflects evolutionary success, and that probability is enhanced by a high-quality environment as required by each particular organism. A plant requiring direct sunlight will compete with others of its kind for the highest position in the forest canopy. Koalas, whose diet consists exclusively of leaves of a particular gum tree, will compete for position on – and possession of – those trees.

In this scheme, evolutionary success can be achieved in two ways. The first is through genetic mutation, such that the mutated organism can better exploit the wellbeing properties of a new environmental niche. The second is to compete successfully within existing environmental niches. Such success is referred to as reproductive fitness and results in the genetic selection of animals with the optimum balance of personal characteristics enabling the three abilities, within each environmental niche.

Over time, both of these processes operate to cause evolutionary change. However, in conditions of environmental stability, new environmental niches become increasingly rare, such that the dominant force for reproductive success is successful competition for quality environments. In these terms, while the specific nature of the environment providing life quality varies among species, the competition for life quality is a fundamental quest of life on earth.

A notable aspect of this description is the use of examples taken from the physical world of tangible objects. Indeed, the traditional measures of human life quality focus entirely on the objective circumstances of living (e.g. Human Development Index, 2007/2008). The attraction of objective variables is that, because they are tangible, they can be measured in familiar ways through frequencies or quantities. Moreover, in the tradition of the physical sciences, the results can be verified by any number of people using the same techniques of measurement. Because of this, objective measures of life quality travel well cross-culturally. For example, medical health can be defined by universal criteria and money can be standardized to American dollars.

Despite these advantages, the use of objective indexes to represent life quality is misleading. Here there are two traditions, one based in economics and the other in medicine. Each assumes that the physical variables which are of primary concern to their discipline have a simple relationship with a global construct, most commonly referred to as wellbeing. This assumption warrants examination.

1.1   Wellbeing

The term 'wellbeing' describes a global conception of life quality (Cummins, 2014). Although this concept is too vague to be matched by a valid form of measurement, as soon as 'wellbeing' is dissected, it separates into objective and subjective variables.

These two categories can then be further subdivided to produce any number of subcategories which, together, represent the entire wellbeing construct. A panoramic example is provided by the Australian Bureau of Statistics (Trewin, 2001), which regards wellbeing in terms of individuals and society, living conditions, social arrangements, and progress towards social goals. These areas then subsume all of the demographic statistics (e.g. unemployment rate) and subjective measures (e.g. are conditions getting better or worse?) measured by that agency. In a similar vein, many omnibus surveys claim to measure wellbeing through the use of both objective and subjective variables. An example is the Australian Unity Wellbeing Index (Cummins et al., 2013c). Crucially, however, none of these methodologies attempts to create a single empirical value for wellbeing, and if they did, the measure would be invalid. The reason is the highly complex and non-linear relation between objective and subjective variables, exemplified by the efforts within medicine and economics to create global measures of wellbeing and life quality.

1.1.1   Wellbeing in Medicine

The medical version of life quality is called Health Related Quality of Life (for a critique of the HRQOL construct, see Cummins, 2010). In this conception an excellent level of HRQOL represents the absence of pathology as reported by the patient. Thus, it has been suggested, HRQOL may be used '[a]s a clinical trial end point ... with a value equal to disease-free survival' (Cella et al., 1993, p. 570).

As examples of this interpretation of HRQOL scale data, both Hildingh and Baigi (2010) and Batinic et al. (2010) measure wellbeing by using the General Health Questionnaire (Goldberg and Williams, 1988). Both sets of authors refer to their results in terms of 'well-being' whereas, in fact, the scale they used is intended as a screening device for identifying minor psychiatric disorders. The 'well-being' that they deduce is based on a low profile for psychiatric disorders. Similarly, Alvarez et al. (2010) describe the output of the WHOQOL-Bref (WHOQOL Group, 1994) as wellbeing, but the scale involves items measuring pathology.

This focus on pathology represents a severe limitation to the usefulness of HRQOL scales in non-pathological samples. Whereas subjective wellbeing (see Section 2) can represent either low or high perceived life quality, because HRQOL scales represent levels of perceived medical pathology, the highest life quality they can yield is the absence of medical pathology. This absence is then interpreted as high life quality for the patient, no matter if they have just separated from their partner, lost their job, and run over the family dog. As an example of this limitation, the most widely used HRQOL instrument is the SF-36 (McHorney et al., 1993). This includes such items as 'limitations in ability to walk 100 meters'. There is, therefore, a clear con-found with life quality as measured by this instrument and global life quality as perceived by the individual. The assump-tion that people confined to a wheelchair necessarily have low subjective life quality as a result of their physical disability is utterly wrong (see e.g. Brickman et al., 1978). In summary, measures of HRQOL are useful as patient-reported outcomes of their pathological symptoms. They are not useful as measures of general wellbeing.

1.1.2   Wellbeing in Economics

The foundations for the discipline of economics are considered to have been laid by the Scottish philosopher Adam Smith (1776, 1869), with the English philosopher, lawyer, and social reformer Jeremy Bentham (1780, 1789) making the connection between economics and population happiness (Burns, 2005). In that era, these authors had no data on which to base their ideas, so they used philosophical assumptions instead. Most crucially for the current discussion, they believed that the subjective benefits of economic activity could not be directly measured. So in order to estimate such benefits, they inferred them from an individual's rational-choice behaviour. This form of benefit became known as 'utility', defined by Bentham (1780, p. 8) as 'that property in any object, whereby it tends to produce benefit, advantage, plea-sure, good, or happiness ... or ... to prevent the happening of mischief, pain, evil, or unhappiness to the party whose interest is considered'.

Bentham considered that this definition applied to both individuals and the community in general. Moreover, because rational choices in economic transactions were more likely to yield monetary advantage than would irrational choices, income or wealth became proxy for happiness. This then allowed the logical conclusion that the more money individuals or nations have, the happier they are.

This was a clever philosophical device at that time. It allowed discussions of the money–happiness relation while avoiding the need to measure happiness directly. Unfortunately, this philosophy has persisted within economics way beyond its use-by date. For example, writing for Bauers's (1966) seminal introduction to social indicators (for an assessment of this work, see Land and Michalos, 2017), one of US President Truman's economics advisors stated that happiness could not be directly measured, and could only be indirectly estimated through 'surrogates', such as through choices made (Gross, 1966).

This view misrepresented the available social sciences literature at that time. Thirty-six years earlier, the psychologist Watson (1930) had reported that self-ratings of happiness on a printed rating scale correlated 0.81 with a composite score comprising a number of subjective indices. Watson had concluded that the general level of happiness could be measured reliably. Numerous other researchers followed his lead, and it was soon discovered that measures of mood happiness were not only reliable but also surprisingly stable over time. For example, Hartmann (1934) obtained a test–retest reliability of 0.70 with two measurements a month apart, while Wessman and Ricks (1966) reported that happiness-related measures taken two years apart correlated 0.67. In summary, the reliable and valid direct measurement of trait happiness has removed this variable from the provinces of both philosophy and economics. Such studies now properly belong in psychology.

1.1.3   Wellbeing in Psychology

Psychological wellbeing is best conceptualized by the Psychological Well-Being Questionnaire (Ryff, 1989), which has sovereign status through its title. This instrument measures the construct through six subscales: self-acceptance, positive relations with others, autonomy, environmental mastery, purpose of life, and personal growth. While these subscales may be useful as separate measures, collectively they are proposed to embody the construct of eudaimonic wellbeing, as opposed to the hedonic construct of wellbeing represented by subjective wellbeing (see Ryan & Deci, 2001). However, since the subscales of the Psychological Well-Being Questionnaire do not reliably factor together (Clarke et al., 2001; Kafka & Kozma, 2002), and because the construct of eudaimonic wellbeing refers mainly to the unmeasurable philosophical ideals of reaching high personal and human potentials (Deci & Ryan, 2008b), attention will now be focussed on the simpler wellbeing construct of subjective wellbeing.

2   Subjective Wellbeing

2.1   An Historical and Contemporary Perspective

Subjective Wellbeing (SWB) has been a topic of scientific study for more than 40 years. While sporadic earlier publications concerned the investigation of happiness, as has been described, it was the remarkable work of Andrews and Withey (1976) and Campbell et al. (1976) that launched the area into scientific prominence. Both texts demonstrated that SWB data could be reliably measured and that statistical analysis, using interval-level data and linear statistics, produced coherent results. Of particular importance, both publications confirmed earlier research showing SWB to be remarkably stable. It has been this stability and reliability of measurement that has made SWB such an attractive new area for subsequent quantitative investigation. Perhaps the most important innovation has been the increasingly common inclusion of SWB in national surveys, which has resulted in the creation of a vast repository of SWB data.

The interpretation of these data, however, has been fraught with difficulties. Two of the most serious and fundamental problems have been the lack of a standardized terminology (see Diener, 2006 for a review) and the huge number of different instruments that claim to measure aspects of SWB (for a listing see ACQOL, 2017). In combination, this lack of standardization in both nomenclature and instrumentation has led to a conceptual jungle.

Perhaps the single most serious problem is with the words *hedonic* and *eudaimonic*. Both were bequeathed to psychological science from the early Greek philosophers, and many lucid reviews of their ancient history are available (e.g. McGill, 1968; Ryan & Deci, 2001). The philosophers of this period conceived subjective life quality as comprising these two dimensions, and the one that most concerns discussions of SWB is hedonic.

The earliest exponent of hedonic theory, Aristippus of Cyrene (435–356 BCE), regarded 'pleasure' as the pleasure of the moment (Fromm, 1947), proposing that pleasure should properly be extracted from all life circumstances. Epicurus (341–270 BCE) made a sensible revision; although continuing to believe that pleasure is the aim of life, he pointed out that 'while every pleasure is in itself good, not all pleasures are to be chosen, since some pleasures cause later annoyances greater than the pleasure itself' (Fromm, 1947, p. 175).

The modern interpretation of 'hedonic' is as 'pleasurable happiness', comprising a dominance of 'pleasure over pain'. This has become the commonly cited definition of happiness within the social sciences literature (e.g. Bunnin & Yu, 2008; Joshanloo, 2013; Olsson et al., 2013). However, there are many alternative and very diverse opinions concerning this definition.

The term 'happiness' has been used as a blanket term to include all positive feelings about the self (Veenhoven, 2010), as a synonym for SWB (Chang & Nayga, 2010), as referring to average levels of positive and negative affect (Seidlitz & Diener, 1993), and as a single affect within the classification system described by the circumplex model of affect (Russell, 2003). Happiness has also been used to imply different temporal durations, as a long-duration positive mood trait (Seidlitz & Diener, 1993), or as a short-duration positive emotion. The latter is consistent with the term 'happy' in common English usage, which refers to a transient, positive state of mind that has been caused by a specific experience, such as a pleasant social interaction (Diener et al., 2004).

Clearly, from these lists, there is no simple way for the reader to know what the author intends to convey by using this term. So a priority requirement for the current text is to define what meaning is intended by 'happiness', and this requires a description of the general area of psychology known as feelings or, more scientifically, affect.

2.2   Defining Affect

The current understanding of affect is based on two basic principles. The first states that affects can be ordered according to the affective circumplex (Russell, 1980). This is a classificatory system in which affects are depicted on the circumference of a circle intersected by two orthogonal axes. The vertical axis depicts levels of arousal, while the horizontal axis depicts levels of pleasantness. The position of each affect on the circumference is then mathematically determined by its relative content of arousal and pleasantness.

The second understanding is that affect can be further classified as emotion or mood. These two affective states are distinguished by the following features:

1. Moods are primitive, genetic in origin, object-free, and chronic (Oatley & Johnson-Laird, 1987). Emotions are complex, acute, affective-cognitive responses to percepts (Russell, 2003).
2. Moods are low-intensity affects; emotions may be high or low intensity.
3. Mood as pathology is recognized as depression. Emotion as pathology is recognized as bipolar disorder.

This theoretical understanding illustrates how the science of affect has developed a far higher level of sophistication than could be achieved through philosophy alone. It also illustrates how this contemporary view of affect from psychology simply does not fit with the philosophical term 'hedonic'. While 'hedonic' is useful to describe an historical, philosophical notion, its use to describe happiness in contemporary psychology is both misleading and confusing.

To summarize, the term 'happiness' in psychological science refers to a single adjective on the affective circumplex. Subjective wellbeing contains the affect of happiness. However, the systematic form of this happiness is mood, and it is the inclusion of mood happiness that gives SWB its special characteristics.

2.3   Defining Subjective Wellbeing

When most authors define SWB, they cite classic publications such as Andrews and Withey (1976) or Diener (1984). These sources recognize happiness as a component of measured SWB. However, they also support the view that SWB additionally comprises high positive affect, low negative affect, and cognition in the form of a global, personal life assessment. This view requires revision. As first demonstrated by Davern et al. (2007) and thrice confirmed using factor analysis and structural equation modelling (Blore et al., 2011; Longo, 2015; Tomyn & Cummins, 2011a), the composition of SWB is dominated by a three-mood composite. In addition to mood happiness, the other two moods are content and alert. This combination of affects is called Homeostatically Protected Mood (HPMood). As the name suggests, the Theory of Subjective Wellbeing Homeostasis proposes that the level of HPMood is genetically set for each person and protected by a homeostatic system of management. This set-point level of HPMood lies at the heart of homeostasis theory.

2.4   Set-Points for Subjective Wellbeing

Set-points of HPMood are a recent discovery (Capic et al., 2018; Cummins et al., 2014a). While their existence had been mooted much earlier by McGue et al. (1993), their critical demonstration came from recognizing that the affective component of each SWB measurement comprises two parts: an unchanging mood together with a changing affective response to percepts. So to demonstrate each mood set-point, the emotion needed to be stripped from each response. The methodology for achieving this separation is described within the two cited publications.

Following such emotion stripping, the resultant mood has the characteristic of a genetically determined, individual difference, such as has been described for other uniquely individual characteristics under genetic control (Buss & Greiling, 1999; Kanai & Rees, 2011; Tavor et al., 2016). Moreover, because HPMood is the result of emotion-stripping SWB, I propose that this mood is the phenotypic marker of the set-point. Such a genetic link has long been expected since twin-studies showed that SWB has a substantial genetic basis (Lykken & Tellegen, 1996; Tellegen et al., 1988). More recently, based on mounting evidence, Røysamb et al. (2014) concluded, in their review, that the genetic evidence is consistent with the idea of a genetically determined set-point for SWB. So the theoretical and empirical evidence linking individual SWB set-points with genetics seems well established, even though the responsible genome is yet to be discovered.

This proposition, and especially the evidence that set-points are genetically determined, has two major consequences for cross-cultural research. First, that all people, no matter their race or culture, are predicted to have their set-point within the same normal range of set-points as described within Australian data (Capic et al., 2017). The rationale is that genetic set-points, in general, are basic hardware for humans and other mammals. They represent the generally optimal level, of whatever variable is under management, in order to achieve normal functioning. While variation in the level of each managed variable can occur on an acute basis to deal with particular demands, on a chronic basis the set-point level remains the target level for adaptive functioning. Thus, in reference to physiology, people living in the tropics have the same set-point for their core body temperature as people living in cold climates. By analogy, there is no reason to expect culture to change the distribution of set-points for SWB.

Second, again consistent with the physiological literature, the most adaptive SWB level for each person is proposed to be the area immediately around their set-point; their set-point-range. This level is achieved, on a chronic basis, through the operation of a homeostatic system which manages affective excursions caused by emotion, bringing affect back to its normal range. I provide an outline of the homeostatic processes below, and have more completely described them elsewhere (Cummins, 2016, 2017).

3   Subjective Wellbeing Homeostasis

Following Cannon (1932) and consistent with the description by McEwen and Wingfield (2003), homeostasis can be defined as *the management of an essential variable to a set-point, representing an optimal level for the operation for each individual*. When forces external to each homeostatic system cause movement of its managed variable away from its set-point, the system generates counteractive measures designed to return the variable to its optimal level. For example, the sensation of feeling cold causes changes in blood distribution and behaviour, both directed to retain more body heat.

All set-points have a normal distribution caused by genetic variation. Within physiology, these distributions are very tight, representing the small margin of variation that is adaptive for the human organism. The set-points for SWB have rather larger variation, with a normal distribution between about 70 to 90 points on the 0–100 point scale (Cummins et al., 2014). This distribution has been confirmed using a different data set from the original (Capic et al., 2017), additionally showing that the set-points are practically identical for both SWB and HPMood. Thus, this essential component for the demonstration of SWB homeostasis is now in place.

Homeostasis Theory (Cummins, 2016) proposes that the level of HPMood is normally managed to lie within its set-point-range for each person. The extent of this range is about eight percentage points on either side of the set-point (Capic et al., 2017). The proposed role of HPMood is to provide each person with a constant, stable, gentle, background level of affective positivity and alertness.

The active component of homeostasis is the system that maintains SWB around its set-point. It is proposed that this system monitors the discrepancy between the set-point level of HPMood and momentary affect from emotion. When a discrepancy is detected, the system strives to return the level of SWB to set-point using a variety of management devices.

3.1   Homeostatic Control

The challenge to homeostatic control comes from emotions. These represent the constantly changing feelings resulting from percepts, and these emotions are normally felt at a level that is stronger than the background HPMood. This differential strength is crucial for the normal operation of our perceptual systems. Because HPMood is a weak background affect, this allows the affect accompanying an emotion to be noticed, as it signals a change in the internal or external environment. This change then demands attention from the cognitive brain processes. In turn, cognitive processing determines whether the cause of the changed affect constitutes a threat or is benign and can be ignored. Thus, during the waking day, attention is constantly being shifted in response to emotion input.

This arrangement is highly adaptive in allowing selective attention to be paid to those aspects of the environment that most need attention. However, in order for the system to remain sensitive to change, the level of affect from each emotional event must be transitory. Were the emotion to persist, its presence would mask other sources of change in the environment, which would generally be maladaptive.

The vast volume of constantly changing emotional input to the brain is mainly generated in response to minor and predictable stimuli, which can be safely ignored. The mechanism by which such environmental changes are recognized as benign is an active brain process.

3.1.1 Habituation

The process of habituation describes decreasing responsiveness to a repeated stimulus (Thompson, 2009). This is not due to sensory adaptation or motor fatigue, but rather is an adaptive behaviour involving a form of primitive learning. Its purpose is to conserve resources by reducing the response to stimuli that are predictable. So, for example, the tick-tock of the bedside clock quickly becomes unnoticed as habituation takes control. Equally, habituation explains why beautiful new shoes soon appear normal as habituation erodes their initial ability to create positive affect.

Habituation can only occur when the stimulus is perceived as innocuous. If the stimulus is perceived as threatening to SWB, then other forms of homeostatic defence are activated. The most obvious of these is to use behaviour.

3.1.2 Behaviour

The most effective defence against an intense emotion that threatens homeostasis is to avoid the cause or, if this is not possible, to disengage as soon as possible (Schulz & Heckhausen, 1996). Life routines assist this process, by reducing the probability of encountering unsought challenges. However, some sources of negative emotion can be neither avoided nor disengaged. An example from individualistic culture is the experience of a devoted primary carer of a disabled family member with behavioural problems (Hammond et al., 2014). Within a collectivist culture, people may be unable to disengage from chronically experienced unpleasant duty to members of the extended family.

Under these conditions, the person must turn to other homeostatic strategies to maintain normal levels of SWB. Some of these strategies use resources acquired from the environment, while others are internal to each person. The three major environmental resources used to facilitate homeostatic control are called the Golden Triangle Resources.

3.2   Golden Triangle Resources

As any adult knows, there are three special resources that facilitate a happy life: money, an intimate relationship, and having a purposeful activity. Each of these resources facilitates homeostasis by meeting a basic need. These three resources are particularly powerful because they have a dual role in facilitating homeostatic control. While their primary function is to defend against homeostatic failure and assist homeostatic recovery, they also generate a feel-good factor when they are engaged. In this they differ from other basic needs, such as safety, which is mainly noticeable in its absence. That is, feeling safe is not a homeostatic buffer; it is neutral as far as homeostasis is concerned. Feeling unsafe, however, is a homeostatic threat.

These three 'golden resources' form the primary external homeostatic buffers. Their further characterization is as follows.

3.2.1   Money

There are serious misconceptions as to what money can and cannot do in relation to SWB. People who are rich experience rapid adaptation to high living standards, so living in a mansion with servants will feel luxurious at first, but over time it will just feel 'normal'. Moreover, high wealth cannot shift the set point to create a perpetually happier person. Set-points for SWB are under genetic control (Braungart et al., 1992; Lykken & Tellegen, 1996), so in this sense, money cannot buy happiness. No matter how rich someone becomes, once their level of income saturates the wealth-dependent buffering capacity of the homeostatic system, additional wealth will not raise SWB further. What this means in practical terms is that no matter how rich someone is, their average level of SWB cannot be sustained higher than within the upper-half of their set-point range.

The real power of wealth is to protect SWB through its capacity as a flexible resource to assist homeostasis (Cummins, 2000). It does this by allowing people to minimize the unwanted challenges they experience in their daily life. Wealthy people pay others to perform tasks they do not wish to do themselves. Thus, the level of SWB rises with income in an asymptotic curve. In terms of national comparisons, poor countries exhibit lower levels of SWB due to the increased incidence of homeostatic failure among people living in poverty (World Bank, 1997).

3.2.2   Relationships

Humans are highly social animals, driven by the long period of childhood dependence during which the probability of child survival is enhanced by adult cooperation. It is therefore not surprising that the most powerful external buffer is a relationship with another person, which provides the feeling of being emotionally supported (see, e.g. Ensel & Lin, 1991), and at best a relationship that involves mutual sharing of intimacies and support (Cummins, Walter & Woerner,, 2007). Almost universally, the research literature attests to the power of intimate relationships (Lowenthal & Haven, 1968) to moderate the influence of potential stressors on SWB (for reviews, see Henderson, 1977; Sarason, 1977; Sarason et al., 1990b).

This relationship resource is more predictably available in collectivist than in individualist cultures. Within the latter, nuclear families reduce the daily involvement of other relatives, and thus make the relationship between partners more critical to supply this homeostatic resource.

3.2.3   Achieving in Life

The process of active engagement, providing purpose in life, is the third golden resource.

A voluminous literature attests to the fact that when people lose this buffer through, for example, unemployment, their SWB is severely threatened (Clark et al., 2008).

In summary, these three resources of money, intimate relationships, and achieving in life are proposed as the universally most important resources to support normal homeostatic control. However, they can only assist homeostatic processes to a limited extent. If a source of challenge is strong and persistent, other homeostatic resources are called into play. These are the cognitive buffers, which are internal to individuals' thoughts about themselves.

3.3   Internal Resources

The cognitive buffers comprise protective internal devices designed to minimize the impact of personal failure on positive feelings about our self. The most important of these is our shifting sense of control.

3.3.1   Secondary Control

Secondary control techniques were first described by Rothbaum et al. (1982), and a detailed discussion in relation to SWB appears in Cummins and Nistico (2002). Secondary control protects SWB against the conscious reality of life. Its role is to minimize the impact of personal failure. Secondary control alters the way we see ourselves in relation to some emotionally challenging agent which is putting homeostatic control at risk. The basic cognitive process is called cognitive restructuring, whereby the memory of the negative event is altered to the advantage of the person.

The ways of thinking that can achieve cognitive restructuring are highly varied. For example, one can find meaning in the event ('God is testing me'), fail to take responsibility for the failure ('It was not my fault.'), or regard the failure (e.g. dropping a vase) as unimportant ('I did not need that old vase anyway'). The consequence of such restructuring is that the negativity of a challenging experience is deflected away from the core view of self. This allows homeostatic control of self-satisfaction to return.

In summary, the combined external and internal buffers ensure that our wellbeing is robustly defended. There is, as a consequence, considerable stability in the SWB of individuals and populations.

3.4 SWB Stability

Given the homeostatic system that has been described, which attempts to keep SWB close to set-point, it might be anticipated that levels of SWB are fairly stable. In fact, as previously mentioned, this phenomenon was noted more than 80 years ago by Hartmann (1934). He measured the 'happiness' of 10th grade students and reported a one-month test–retest reliability of 0.70. However, it was another 50 years before estimates of SWB stability were used to develop normal ranges, and these concerned the stability of population means rather than the SWB levels of individuals.

In 1995, Cummins used the mean scores of 'life satisfaction', derived from population surveys, as data. These results were all derived from Western populations but, in other respects, had a very heterogeneous origin. Each survey had been conducted by different researchers, using different scales of measurement, at different times over the decades 1970–1990. The key to combining these disparate results was to convert all mean scores to the standardized 0–100 range called 'percentage of Scale Maximum' (%SM). The formula for this conversion appears in the manual for the Personal Wellbeing Index (International Wellbeing Group, 2013).

When the mean scores from the 16 population surveys were recoded to lie in the 0–100 percentage point range, they averaged 75 points, and their standard deviation was 2.5. These 16 survey mean scores were then used as data to create a normative range. Two standard deviations on either side of the 'mean of the means' creates a range within which there is a 95% probability of including any particular survey mean. This procedure yielded a normal range of 70–80 points and represents the first estimation of a normal range for SWB population mean scores.

This, however, is a very approximate estimation, heavily contaminated with error variance resulting from the many methodological differences between the studies. Much greater stability has been revealed by the 31 surveys conducted up to September 2014 through the Australian Unity Wellbeing Index project. This project samples 2,000 fresh respondents several times each year. People are recruited by telephone, from the Australian adult population, by random dialling within 50 specified geographic regions that together cover the continent. Sampling within each region is proportional to population density.

Using the mean scores of these 31 surveys as data, the grand mean is 75.3 points and the standard deviation 0.72. This yields a normative range of 73.8–76.7 points. In other words, the mean score of a random survey of people in Australia can be predicted, with 95% certainty, to lie within a 2.9 percentage point range.

Anglim et al. (2015) provided a sophisticated confirmation of SWB stability at the level of individual people. The data were provided from a longitudinal survey of Australian adults (n = 1,081) who provided semi-annual SWB scores on between 5 and 10 occasions. Using Bayesian hierarchical modelling and SWB levels measured by the Personal Wellbeing Index (International Wellbeing Group, 2013), the mean was 75.0 points with an average within-person standard deviation of 6.60 points. The test–retest correlation at 7+ years with the first year yielded r = 0.76. Within the whole sample, SWB for each person generally fluctuated between about 2.0 or 3.0 percentage points on either side of 75.0 points. There is no precedent in the literature for such extraordinary stability in measures of SWB. In a global context, however, there is much greater variation.

When the population mean scores from non-Western countries are examined, it is evident that there is considerably more variation than I have so far described (Cummins, 1998). Countries differ in wealth, and the relation between national wealth and SWB has been well documented (World Bank, 1997). However, while there is certainly a strong overall relation between national wealth and SWB, this relation is not linear. That is, there is more going on to change national levels of SWB than just variations in national income. For example, countries with uniformly low income vary widely in their level of average SWB. This indicates that population SWB can be heavily influenced by many other national factors such as civil disturbance, food shortage, disease, bad governance, and the like. Importantly, measured levels of SWB may also vary according to culture.

4   Cross-Cultural Differences in SWB

4.1   Introduction

When researchers find that the level of SWB differs between cultural groups, they often interpret their result literally (e.g. 'Americans have higher happiness than Japanese'). While such a simplistic interpretation was acceptable in decades past, due to poor understanding of the SWB construct, today such conclusions are at odds with a large and sophisticated literature.

A vast repository of international research now evidences many confounding factors regarding reported levels of SWB, making the validity of direct SWB comparisons between countries either uncertain or invalid. One of these is the ways that people from different cultures process, and respond to, the questions used to measure SWB. As concluded more than 20 years ago by Veenhoven (1996), respondents can vary in their interpretations of certain words, their understanding of the intended meaning of a question, or their conceptualization of an entire scale due to differences in language or in cultural assumptions. Such divergent processing of information may then cause systematic response biases, which lead to non-equivalent constructs across cultural groups (Bieda et al., 2017). However, before exploring these issues, the meaning of 'culture' must be clarified.

An authoritative definition of a 'cultural group' is offered by Merriam-Webster (2018) as 'the customary beliefs, social forms, and material traits of a racial, religious, or social group'. So in these terms culture may be viewed as a key part of each child's developmental environment. Within each culture, children are taught a common code of what to believe and how to properly interact with other people, and they undertake this learning in a shared demographic and social environment. In addition to experiential learning, it is also possible that, through epigenetic mechanisms, culture moulds a child's gene expression for some culture-specific traits. That is, key factors influencing cultural learning do so by modifying gene expression, without altering the genetic information (Berger et al., 2009; National Institutes of Health, 2017).

As a result of these developmental influences, adults display both individual and collective psychological characteristics. Their individuality is the product of a unique genetic endowment and experiential history. Their shared characteristics with others derive from common genetic traits and a shared cultural experience. These shared characteristics define a person as having the behavioural and belief characteristics of a cultural group, consistent with the Merriam-Webster definition. This description of culture is relevant to the interpretation of SWB measurement.

As I described earlier, levels of SWB are known to be susceptible to the availability of homeostatic resources. However, this is not the only reason for variation in SWB between countries. Differential cultural training may be another. Most particularly within the current context, culture teaches people to respond to personal questions with various levels of caution. For example, while Australians feel free to report how they really feel, people living in a repressive regime have learned to temper their response to conform to societal expectations.

As a result of this response training, when countries are compared with one another, there are two sources of systematic influences on measured SWB. In addition to the level of homeostatic support through the three golden domains, there is also cultural response bias, of uncertain strength and valence.

This dual influence makes the interpretation of SWB differences between countries uncertain. Moreover, since this bias is observed in the data provided by SWB scales of measurement, it raises the issue of whether such data validly represent the SWB construct. This uncertainty will persist until the character of the response bias is described and quantified.

These complex issues will be explored in four stages:

First, to provide background understanding regarding the nature of
    SWB and differences between cultures relevant to the provision
    of SWB data.
Second, to identify the simplest, most reliable and valid scales to
    represent SWB.
Third, to examine the statistical character of cultural response bias
    through the use of measurement invariance.
Finally, to speculate on a hypothetical study designed to determine
    the influence of cultural response bias in SWB measurement.

4.2   *Measuring Subjective Wellbeing*

The number of scales claiming to measure SWB is bewildering.
Driven by a lack of agreement regarding the nature of SWB, there
are many differing opinions as to what questions should be asked
to measure the construct. This has stimulated a considerable
number of researchers to devise their own scale and their legacy
is a huge collection of disparate instruments described by the
Australian Centre on Quality of Life (ACQOL, 2017).

This diversity would be interesting if the instruments were psychometrically sound, measuring well-defined and theoretically
embedded views of SWB. Unfortunately, this is generally not so.
So a decision must be taken as to which scales offer the best
potential for providing an agreed, basic measure of SWB in order
to examine cross-cultural differences. The selection has been
strongly influenced by scale validity and simplicity.

4.2.1   Basic Measures of Subjective Wellbeing

Looking through the long list of SWB measures provided by the
Australian Centre on Quality of Life (ACQOL, 2017) it is evident
that most scales attempt to measure the construct through inclu-
siveness and complexity. They employ many items to achieve a
broad coverage of subjective life experience, with the items
formed into sub-scales. Such instruments are not an efficient
way to investigate cross-cultural understanding of SWB for three
reasons.

First, such scales will inevitably show that the data derived from two cultures are different from one another. But the interpretation of this difference will be uncertain. Not only are there no norms by which to establish whether one or both sets of data lie within normal ranges, but also there is no theory to guide expected data variation under different cultural conditions.

Second, the more items that are used in a SWB scale, the higher the probability that some items are more relevant to one culture than the other, rather than being generic measures of SWB. Not only will such items confound the creation of a common measurement scale, but their cultural specificity will take the measured construct away from the personal-abstract dimension that lies at the heart of SWB (Cummins et al., 2003).

Third, the likelihood that a multi-factor scale will show measurement invariance between cultures is extremely low (see later).

The alternative to using complex scales is to use the simplest possible scales to measure SWB. If it can be demonstrated that the simplest scales measure the core of SWB, then such measures must represent the best chance of demonstrating cross-cultural validity.

In summary, it is predicted that, using the simplest forms of SWB measurement, SWB data collected within any cultural group will display the following characteristics: SWB will behave as though it is under the influence of a homeostatic system of control. This will involve, inter alia, evidence of set-points, temporal stability, normative ranges for data at both the individual and population level, resource saturation such that increasing levels of any homeostatic resource demonstrate an asymptotic relationship with levels of SWB, and predictable positive or negative relations with relevant other variables.

These characteristics can be most reliably observed in data from three scales representing the simplest forms of SWB measurement. These are Global Life Satisfaction (GLS; Andrews & Withey, 1976), the Satisfaction with Life Scale (SWLS; Diener et al., 1985), and the Personal Wellbeing Index (PWI; International Wellbeing Group, 2013). I will now describe each of these measures.

4.2.2   Global Life Satisfaction (GLS)

The simplest form of rating scale, with which to measure subjective wellbeing (SWB), is a single question asking about global life satisfaction (GLS). The earliest form of such a scale, converting general subjective impressions into empirical data, emerged almost 100 years ago when Freyd (1923) published his Graphic Rating Scale (see Cummins & Gullone, 2000). Intended to assist the evaluative rating of job candidates, the scale comprised an unmarked horizontal line under which were five graded descriptions of, for example, the candidate's general appearance. The interviewers were instructed: 'When you have satisfied yourself on the standing of this person in the trait on which you are rating him, place a check at the appropriate point on the horizontal line. You do not have to place your check directly above a descriptive phrase. You may place your check at any point on the line' (p. 88). Freyd recommended scoring the responses by dividing the line into 10 or 20 equal intervals.

A few years later, Watson (1930) published a similar scale to measure trait happiness, with such instructions to respondents as 'Comparing yourself with other persons of the same age and sex, how do you feel you should rate your own general happiness?' He also used an unmarked horizontal line with five descriptors placed underneath; however, these were anchored at each extreme by 'Most miserable of all' and 'Happiest of all', with three intermediate descriptors, and the mid-point labelled 'The average person of your own age and sex'. Watson had introduced the bipolar scale with a neutral mid-point. Importantly, the descriptors were intended only as approximate guides, and each respondent made their own mark to indicate the precise level of their 'own general happiness'. Responses were then scored from 0 to 100, and Watson found the mean score of 388 graduate students to be 71.8 percentage points, which is a good approximation to normal contemporary SWB estimates (Cummins et al., 2013, table A2.21).

A short time later, Likert (1932) changed the face of subjective measurement by introducing his five-choice response scale. This drastically reduces the number of effective choice-points, because the scoring system is no longer continuous. Respondents are required to mark the line only adjacent to one of the categorical labels, making the scoring system 1–5. This format endures today, with its popularity due to simplicity and face validity. However, an even further reduction in response choice was introduced by Gurin et al. (1960) in the form of a three-level choice: 'Taking things all together, how would you say things are these days – would you say you're very happy, pretty happy, or not too happy these days?' (p. 19). It is unfortunate that this scale also gained great popularity, most especially within national surveys, as this format creates a very blunt instrument by which to detect change (for a review, see Cummins and Gullone, 2000).

A return to greater scale sensitivity came with Andrews and Withey's (1976, p. 66) seven-choice 'Delighted–Terrible' response scale. Respondents were asked, 'How do you feel about your life as a whole?' and provided with an expanded Likert-type scale, anchored by 'Terrible' and 'Delighted', with five intermediate adjectives. The authors cite compelling evidence (p. 86) that their seven-point response scales provide more sensitive indications of respondents' feelings than do the three-point scales.

However, even a bipolar, seven-point response scale does not satisfy the theoretical sensitivity that can be achieved by respondents making value judgements on a continuum (Miller, 1956). The reason is that all SWB data display a natural negative skew when measured using either unipolar or bi-dimensional scales (Watson, 1930; Cummins, 1997b). Consequently, the majority of respondents are using only the higher or positive half of the scale in order to register their judgement.

The creation of Likert-type scales with more than seven choice points is difficult due to there being insufficient adjectives to appropriately label the additional choice-points. This barrier was overcome by the creation of end-defined scales, pioneered by Jones and Thurstone (1955). They generated a nine-point scale in relation to food preference, anchored by 'greatest like/dislike' (+4/–4), with a central category of 'Neither like nor dislike' (0), and with the intermediate categories labelled only by their appropriate integer.

An initial concern with providing so many response categories was that they might produce data different from conventionally labelled Likert scales. However, this concern was put to rest by Matell and Jacoby (1972), who used end-defined scales to measure civic beliefs, with the number of numerically defined response choices varying from 2 to 19. Apart from the fact that testing time increased with more than 12-choice formats, no differences were found on the proportions of scale utilized. Similarly, Wyatt and Meyers (1987), using a five-point scale, and Dixon et al. (1984), using a six-point scale, found no systematic differences between the data from end-defined and conventional Likert scales. From this it can be concluded that the end-defined format seems not to bias the data in any particular way.

In the contemporary literature, it is heartening to note that an increasing number of authors are using 10-choice (1 to 10) or 11-choice (0 to 10) end-defined scales. Their decision is reinforced by numerous demonstrations that such scales are generally superior to any other configuration. As examples of this endorsement, Casas (2016) recommends the 0-to-10 format stating that it 'lies within the common experience of children and adolescents (and adults) in most countries and produces increased sensitivity of the measurement instrument' (p. 11). Moreover, Leung (2011), using student respondents in Macau, demonstrated that an 11-point scale produces data closer to interval scaling and normality than do more compressed scales.

In summary, GLS has many of the qualities defining an ideal measure of SWB with which to compare cultural groups. Responses are normally dominated by HPMood but can reflect an emotional takeover from homeostasis if the emotion is strong. Thus, the normal range of GLS under non-threating conditions is a reasonable approximation to set-points. GLS is also ideal in its wording, as proximal to the abstracted self (Cummins et al., 2003), and the 11-point, end-defined response scale allows a reasonable level of sensitivity for the great majority of the population who have a level of SWB between 50 and 100 points. It also has a drawback, however, in being a single item. This precludes estimates of cross-cultural validity through such techniques as measurement invariance. The next two scales both overcome this limitation by having multiple items.

4.2.3   Satisfaction with Life Scale

The Satisfaction with Life Scale (SWLS; Diener et al., 1985) is designed to measure general life satisfaction through the use of five items. It is the most widely used multi-item scale to measure SWB. At the time of this writing the SWLS scale had an h-Index of 261 and more than 360,000 citations. For reviews of the scale, see Pavot and Diener (1993). Each item is phrased to involve an overall judgement of life in general. Thus, the SWLS represents an expanded version of the single-item GLS scale. The SWLS items are not designed to give individual insights into the structure of SWB. This feature makes it different from the Personal Wellbeing Index (International Wellbeing Group, 2013) where each item represents a domain of life which can be separately analysed.

Each of the five SWLS items is rated on a seven-choice response scale, producing a scale score range of 5–35 points. The scale is available from http://internal.psychology.illinois.edu/~ediener/SWLS.html.

Respondents use a seven-point scale anchored by 'strongly disagree' to 'strongly agree'.

The items are as follows:

1. In most ways my life is close to my ideal.
2. The conditions of my life are excellent.
3. I am satisfied with my life.
4. So far I have gotten the important things I want in life.
5. If I could live my life over, I would change almost nothing.

Basic Psychometrics Properties

It is generally agreed that the SWLS scale is internally reliable and that the five items can be combined into one underlying dimension measuring GLS (e.g. Moksnes et al., 2014; Silva et al., 2015; van

Beuningen, 2012). The scale also displays two issues of psycho-metric concern as follows:

Extreme wording: The wording of items tends to be extreme. Most likely due to this construction, people are reticent to give full endorsement as 'strongly agree', so they avoid this highest response category. As a consequence, the SWLS produces a lower average value than the Personal Wellbeing Index, and with a larger variance. For example in a sample of college students (Renn et al., 2009), the mean SWLS and PWI are reported as 72.0 and 75.4, respectively, with standard deviations of 17.0 and 13.9. A similar or greater level of difference has been commonly reported by other authors (e.g. Bedin & Sarriera, 2015; Holton et al., 2010).

Complex wording: van Beuningen (2012) investigated why, in their general population sample, the correlation between GLS and SWLS was not very strong (0.56) and discovered a sub-group of respondents who misinterpreted some of the SWLS items. These people had either low levels of education or were non-native speakers. When these respondents were removed, the correlation increased to 0.66. The authors concluded that the wording of the SWLS might be too complex for general use.

Other authors agree, especially in relation to items 4 and 5. For example, Moksnes et al. (2014) collected data on Norwegian adolescents 13–18 years of age and concluded that the correlated residual variances between these two items implies the adolescents had difficulty in differentiating their semantic meaning. They also note that these two items refer to the past, thereby involving a different response strategy than for the other three items of the scale, which focus on the present. This difference had also been noted by Pavot and Diener (1993). An additional issue has been noted by Oishi (2006) in relation to item 5, which uses counterfactual reasoning. This involves complex cognitive processing and is likely to be difficult to translate (for an extended discussion, see Bloom, 1981).

Potential for a simplified scale

From the preceding discussion it is evident that items 4 and 5 are harder to understand than the other items. In addition, Moksnes et al. (2014) found that allowing the residual variance for items 4 and 5 to correlate caused improved fit.

Were these two items to be removed, the question arises whether this would affect the scale validity. The answer is likely in the negative. The SWLS items are all similar in their relation to GLS, since all aim to ask about 'life in general'. Thus, because it has been established that GLS dominantly comprises HPMood (Capic et al.,2018; Cummins et al., 2014a), it is reasonable to expect that this HPMood dominance applies to each of the SWLS items as well. If this is so, the shared variance of HPMood explains why the items form a tight single factor and also suggests considerable redundancy among the items in terms of representing a single construct of life satisfaction. So, if the two complex items are removed from the scale to produce a three-item version of the SWLS, the validity of the scale is likely to be minimally affected and the items are sufficient in number to form a factor.

The move to a SWLS-3 is given additional impetus when the psychometric performance of the full scale is considered in relation to cross-cultural measurement invariance. This will be given further consideration after the next scale in the triad has been described.

Summary: The advantage of the SWLS over the single GLS item is a higher level of measurement reliability. However, two of the items, numbers 4 and 5, are too complex to be easily understood by some adolescents and adults.

4.2.4   Personal Wellbeing Index

The Personal Wellbeing Index (PWI: International Wellbeing Group, 2013) is designed to measure subjective wellbeing (SWB) through questions of personal satisfaction with the key domains of life. At the time of this writing the scale had an h-Index of 65 and over 17,000 citations.

Construction:

In theoretical terms, the PWI items comprise the most parsi-monious, first-level deconstruction of global life satisfaction (GLS). In empirical terms, each item (domain) must contribute unique as well as shared variance to the prediction of GLS. This is determined through multiple regression. When GLS is simultaneously regressed against all seven domains, the sr^2 statistic represents the proportion of unique variance contrib-uted by each domain. It is calculated as the square of the 'Part' statistic that can be requested from SPSS in association with a multiple regression. When this value is multiplied by 100, it gives the percentage of unique variance contributed by each domain.

The history of scale development is available in the scale man-ual. The current fifth edition has seven core domains as: standard of living, health, achieving in life, relationships, safety, community-connectedness, and future security. An additional domain of spiri-tuality/religion is optional.

Respondents use an 11-point, unipolar, end-defined scale ran-ging from 'no satisfaction at all' (0) to 'completely satisfied' (10). The average domain score is the measure of SWB and all results are recoded onto a standard 0–100-point distribution. Each domain may also be separately analysed as a measure of satisfaction with that specific life aspect.

The PWI items are as follows:

How satisfied are you with:

1. your standard of living?
2. your health?
3. what you are achieving in life?
4. your personal relationships?
5. how safe you feel?
6. feeling part of your community?
7. your future security?
8. your spirituality or religion? (optional)

Basic Psychometric Properties

It is generally agreed that the scale is internally reliable and that the seven domains can be combined into one underlying dimension measuring SWB (e.g. Cummins et al., 2012; Renn et al., 2009; Tiliouine et al., 2006; van Beuningen & de Jonge, 2011). The seven domains in combination normally account for some 45–50% of the variance in GLS (International Wellbeing Group, 2013).

Of this common variance, around 70% is shared and 30% unique. I suggest that the source of this shared variance is Homeostatically Protected Mood (HPMood), which dominates the composition of SWB (Blore et al., 2011; Davern et al., 2007; Tomyn & Cummins, 2011). The source of the unique variance is the specific cognitive/affective component of each domain triggered by the domain target word.

PWI domains

Using the combined general population survey data from the Australian Unity Wellbeing Index, involving 16 consecutive surveys conducted between 2006 and 2014, Cummins et al. (2013c) pro-vided tables showing the contribution of individual domains to GLS (Appendix Table A 2.17.1, N = 57,580). The seven PWI domains together account for 53.33% of the GLS variance. Of this total, 38.31% is shared variance and 15.04 is unique. Of this unique variance, the strongest three contributors are Standard (5.73%), Achieving (5.03%), and Relationships (2.93%). In sum, these add to 13.96%, or 91.02% of the total unique variance. No other domain contributed more than 0.5% unique variance.

The manual for the PWI shows the results of similar regression analyses conducted using general population data from Algeria, Argentina, Hong Kong, Slovakia, and The Netherlands. The overall average domain contribution of unique variance shows the same sequence as for Australia (Standard 7.6%, Achieving 2.6%, and Relationships 1.6%). However, the individual countries show much variation. The only consistent domain is Standard, which makes the strongest contribution in all of the regressions. The contributions of the other domains, however, are inconsistent.

Summary: The advantage of the PWI over the single GLS item is a higher level of measurement reliability. However, the design intention, that all domains will make a contribution of unique variance to GLS, is not supported by any of the analyses accessed.

4.2.5   GLS versus SWLS versus PWI

The single item of General Life Satisfaction (GLS) has given rise to two derivative scales. The Satisfaction with Life Scale (SWLS) comprises five items which are all variations on GLS, while the Personal Wellbeing Index (PWI) comprises seven items, each of which is designed to share significant unique variance with GLS. Thus, since each of these 13 items requests a self-report by the respondent, concerning a semi-abstract evaluation of their life, it might be expected that they would all share considerable common variance in the form of HPMood. The high correlations among these three scales have been confirmed as follows:

GLS vs SWLS: Anglim et al. (2015): 0.77; van Beuningen (2012): 0.66
GLS vs PWI: Anglim et al. (2015): 0.78; Casas et al. (2009a): 0.60
PWI and SWLS: Anglim et al. (2015): 0.75; Renn et al. (2009): 0.78

4.2.6   Summary

Each of these three scales has acceptable psychometric properties. Moreover, as predicted by their common HPMood content, they all share some 40–50% of their variance. These three scales are therefore strong candidates to represent reliable and valid measures of SWB. Their suitability to provide valid, comparative, cross-cultural data will now be examined.

5   Applying Basic SWB Measures to Cross-Cultural Comparisons

5.1   *Overview*

Within the Western media it is common to find reports that compare the levels of SWB or happiness between countries. The assumption in such reports is that the data being compared are valid between cultures, such that the differences represent meaningful international comparisons of subjective life quality. Three of the most influential surveys, providing data for numerous researchers, are as follows:

(a) The World Happiness Report (Helliwell et al., 2017), ranks 155 countries by their happiness levels. This report was released at the United Nations at an event celebrating the International Day of Happiness. (b) The World Database of Happiness (Veenhoven, 2017) comprises, at the time of writing, 15,485 correlational findings involving happiness, observed in 2,044 studies, excerpted from 1,559 publications. (c) The OECD (2017b) Better Life Index rates around 40 countries on general life satisfaction (GLS).

All of these reports present incongruous results which tend to be ignored. The most obvious come from comparisons of SWB from East Asia compared to Western countries. Consider, for example, the comparisons between Japan and Australia, taken from the latest World Happiness Report (Helliwell et al., 2017). Standardizing the SWB results to the 0–100 percentage point scale, the level of SWB in Japan is 59 points, compared to 73 points for Australia. The authors evidence little surprise at this discrepancy between two countries with developed economies. Neither do they comment on the similarity between SWB levels of Japan (59 points) and Nicaragua (60 points). They simply comment next to each country's result: 'Such measures, while subjective, are a useful complement to objective data to compare the quality of life across countries.' Well, not really. Referring to the Human Development Index (2017), which is an entirely objective index dominated by economics, in the world rankings, Japan rates considerably higher (rank 17) than does Nicaragua (rank 125). From such comparisons it is not clear how to interpret the 'complementary' nature of these objective and subjective comparisons of life quality other than as independent dimensions.

Comparisons of SWB levels between groups can only be valid if the measurement scale performs in precisely the same way within each group. The authors of the cited reports assume such equivalence. However, this assumption is challenged by numerous and converging lines of evidence, which indicate why cross-national comparisons of SWB levels are invalid. These include issues of language translation and the moulding of values and response biases by culture. Confirmatory evidence comes from advanced statistical analyses showing that the performance of scales measuring SWB is not invariant between countries. These issues will now be elaborated.

5.2   Problems of Translation

This problem is simply stated – there is no necessary equivalence between the terms used to construct SWB questionnaires in different languages. Two examples come from the two scales highlighted in this review. Within the Personal Wellbeing Index Item #6 asks, 'How satisfied are you with feeling part of your community?' The understanding of 'community' in Anglophone countries is a broad construct that can refer to neighbourhoods, but also to scattered collectives such as research communities. Within collectivist cultures, however, 'community' refers more specifically to a geographic grouping. These differences cause the item to be non-invariant between cultures (see, e.g. Żemojtel-Piotrowska et al., 2017).

The second example comes from the Satisfaction with Life Scale. Item #5 asks how strongly the respondent agrees that 'If I could live my life over, I would change almost nothing'. Oishi (2006) found this item to be problematic using a cross-cultural, Item Response Theory analysis. He notes that answering the item requires counterfactual reasoning. While this process is commonly employed in Western cultures, it is far more unusual in Chinese cultures (Bloom, 1981), and may therefore present uncertain meaning in translation.

5.3   Culture Moderating Values

Many research papers address the correlation between SWB and other variables, such as with work life and family life. Yet because cultures differ in the emphasis they put on each of these variables, different cultures exhibit systematically different correlations. These, in turn, influence the relationship between work life, family life, and SWB. Thus, the nature and strength of the connection between almost any life aspect and SWB will be at least somewhat dependent on culture. These cultural differences may also influence the actual reported level of SWB, but more importantly, they will certainly affect the internal validity of multi-item measurement scales.

Two examples will serve to make this point. The first involves religion. There are clear differences in the core values espoused by the different religious teachings, and these differences are reflected in the relation between the religious beliefs and SWB. For example, Lavric and Flere (2008) found that not only the strength but also the direction of the correlation between positive affect and religious beliefs varies with religious culture.

As a second example, cultures differ in the level of social capital that they support, and social capital is an effective moderator of common mental disorders (for reviews, see deSilva et al., 2005; deSilva et al., 2007). Social capital at the level of families, called *familism*, is described by strong feelings of loyalty, reciprocity, and solidarity among family members (Marin & Marin, 1991). It concerns support provided by the family collective to one another, one's obligations to the family, and the involvement of relatives with the family (Sabogal et al., 1987). So it should be no surprise that the level of familism is an important factor when considering the relation between caring for a disabled family member and SWB (Aranda & Knight, 1997; Magilvy et al., 2000; Shurgot & Knight, 2004). As a specific demonstration, Latina mothers, higher in familism, are less likely to report negative aspects of caregiving than are non-Latina White mothers (Magana & Smith, 2006). Thus, culture moderates the link between caring for a disabled child and mothers' SWB.

In summary, the problems of equivalence in translation and cultural modification of values put international comparisons of SWB on shaky ground. But an even larger threat to the validity of cultural comparisons comes from cultures teaching their children particular styles of responding to personal questions.

5.4   Cultural Response Bias

Teaching children how to behave and think in ways that are socially sanctioned is the essence of acculturation. As a consequence, people from different cultures show systematic differences in the way they present themselves to others. Qualitative reports through the centuries have described such differences. The word 'gasconade', meaning exaggerated boasting, refers to the citizens of Gascony in southwestern France, who have proverbially been regarded as prone to bragging (Merriam-Webster, 2018). Traditional Japanese children, on the other hand, are taught that bragging is unseemly, and modesty is the essence of good manners (Iwata et al., 1995).

So it is logical to expect that cultural exposure modifies each child's natural response tendencies in systematic ways. Of special relevance to empirical research in SWB is the way people are culturally predisposed to express their feelings about themselves. This especially concerns the extent to which they are willing to match strongly positive feelings about themselves with an extreme category on a response scale. It therefore seems reasonable to expect that people who have been acculturated to behave in a modest manner would be inhibited from describing themselves as 'completely satisfied' with their life, even if that were how they actually felt themselves to be.

People who have been acculturated in a Confucianism-influenced society exhibit this moderating tendency, being inclined to hold back from registering extreme scores (for an interesting review of this tendency within a Confucian culture, see Kim et al., 2008). In contrast, such a tendency would be less evident among people who have been raised in a Western culture.

Empirical evidence for this Confucian response bias has been well documented (e.g. Lee et al., 2002; Stening & Everett, 1984).

Essentially, when data are compared between equivalent demographic groups, people from East Asian cultures rate themselves lower on measures of wellbeing when compared to people from Western cultures. The reasons people display this bias has been elucidated through the use of both quantitative and open-ended questions by Lau, Cummins, and McPherson (2005). These researchers found that respondents in Hong Kong explained their avoidance of extremely positive personal evaluations through a combination of modesty, concern at tempting the fates by rating oneself too high, and having a view that the scale maximum is aspirational rather than actually experienced.

As a consequence of this response bias, samples from East Asian cultures tend to report lower average levels of SWB. That is, people tend to respond 7 or 8 (on a 0–10 scale) and avoid the higher response categories which are more commonly used by people in Western cultures. The operation of this bias then gives the appearance that, on average, people from these cultures have lower levels of SWB than do people from the West.

5.5 Summary

According to Homeostasis Theory, the challenges and resources which influence levels of SWB are quite separate from the cultural factors which affect levels of reported SWB. For example, raising national wealth will, ceteris paribus, lift more people out of poverty, thereby allowing them to achieve better homeostatic control, and so to experience higher levels of SWB. However, there is no reason to expect culture, of itself, to influence homeostatic control over SWB. Extant mainstream cultures have all been successful in nurturing our species. Presumably, therefore, all extant cultures allow their members to have an average level of SWB that approximates the average set-point. Moreover, because set-points are hypothesized to represent a genetically determined individual difference, which has an assumed standard distribution within the world's people, all cultural groups should have the same resting level of SWB.

In summary, if the variance in SWB caused by the balance between homeostatic challenges and resources was to be equalized, cultural differences in levels of SWB should disappear. But they do not. So the reason that culture associates with measured cross-cultural differences is proposed to be cultural response bias. However, this is a hypothetical construct based on inference, since no direct measure of the bias has yet been made. Further understanding of this phenomenon can be achieved, however, by statistically detailing the responses to SWB questions.

6 Measurement Invariance

6.1 Introduction

Most of the scales used to measure SWB are multi-item, and their observed mean score is the basic statistic used to compare cross-cultural groups. However, the validity of such comparisons is dependent on a major assumption, which is that the people from the different cultural groups are responding to the scale items in the same way. To the contrary, however, it is very likely that different cultural groups respond differently to a standard scale. The many reasons to expect such response differences have already been discussed. So now it is time to turn to statistics for help in specifying these various influences, and one of the most powerful tools for this purpose is measurement invariance. This technique meticulously examines a hierarchy of steps in comparing the ways that responses to scale items form factors, with each step more stringent than the one before. The result provides a determination of whether, and to what extent, the latent construct measured by each factor is validly represented by the observed factor mean scores. Thus, this statistical technique has the potential to take cross-cultural research to a new level by determining what kinds of questionnaire items can and cannot be used to validly compare the mean scores of any two cultural groups.

The application of this statistic takes the requirement for valid measurement equivalence beyond the demonstration of accurate translation into the language of each cultural group. It also takes the criterion of valid scale composition beyond simple factor analysis. In order for the numerical comparison of observed factor means to be valid between different groups, measurement invariance requires that those groups have responded to the same set of questions in the same way. While invariance testing has been available for more than three decades (Drasgow, 1987; Drasgow & Kanfer, 1985), it is still not commonly employed, likely due to its statistical sophistication.

The basis of invariance testing lies in factor analysis, which remains the most commonly used demonstration of validity in the cross-cultural literature. Factor analysis provides an estimate of how well the items forming each scale relate to one another. It does this by searching for correlations involving unobserved 'latent factors'. In the case of sub-scales, it shows the extent to which items relate more strongly to those in their own sub-scale, compared to items in a different sub-scale.

Each latent factor represents the strongest set of multiple inter-correlations within a scale, formed by statistically grouping the observed variables in multiple ways. In this analytic process, the scale items are modelled as linear combinations of the potential latent factors, plus 'error' terms (the deviation of the observed values from their true theoretical values). The aim of factor analysis is to find independent latent factors. A perfect solution would be an outcome where both the observed and latent factor means of each discovered factor were identical, and there was no error term. In practice, the validity of a factor analysis is measured by the extent to which this ideal is met.

The above description applies to a factor analysis conducted on scores from a single group of people. When the scores of two or more groups are compared, as in cross-cultural comparisons, an additional requirement is that the factor structures, factor loadings, and error terms are equivalent *between* the groups being compared. To elaborate, factor loadings represent regressions of observed variables on the latent variables. If these factor loadings are equivalent across groups, then the observed variables are equally saturated with the latent variable, or at least related in the same way to the latent variable, across the relevant groups. When this occurs, the scale is working in the same way for members of both groups. This is the fundamental cornerstone for regarding differences between groups on observed factor scores as valid.

Importantly, however, such correlations and factor loadings will vary from one data set to another, especially between different cultural groups. Respondents from different cultures are likely to respond to SWB scale items in different ways, as has been discussed. This is not just in the different strength of their registered feeling about the item, but also in the differing relations between one scale item and another. Thus, these differing relations are very likely to produce a mismatch between the observed factor scores and the latent factor scores. When this occurs, the observed scores being compared are an invalid representation of the construct the researcher intends to compare between the groups.

This understanding has huge ramifications for interpreting the extant literature. Almost universally, reviews comparing SWB levels across cultures comprise results for which factorial invariance has not been demonstrated (see, e.g. Oishi, 2010; Cummins, 1998). Thus, the conclusions drawn from such reviews are called into question. Only if the requirement for factorial invariance is met can the observed factor scores between two groups be considered to represent valid estimates of group difference.

In summary, meeting the conditions of measurement invariance is necessary to conclude that a difference between the observed factor scores across cultural groups is valid. Invariance requires not only that both groups of people have responded to an equivalent measurement instrument but also that they have responded to the instrument using the same response style.

6.2 *Estimating Invariance*

In order for the observed factor means to validly represent the latent factors in comparisons of cross-cultural groups, the statistical composition (measurement structure) of the factors, as generated by the respondents' data, must be the same between the comparison groups. Thus, the observed item scores must have an identical statistical relation with the latent variable within each of the groups being compared (see Meredith, 1993). In other words, the responses forming the measurement structure must not be dependent on their group membership. They must be 'invariant,' and there are two commonly employed ways to measure this property.

6.2.1   Item Response Theory

IRT is analogous to Confirmatory Factor Analysis and can be used to determine item bias between groups, as first proposed by Mellenbergh (1989). This bias refers to the way people from two separate groups respond to the same scale item. Tests of Differential Item Functioning (DIF) estimate this bias for each item, and if they are equivalent, the scale can be considered invariant. A good description of DIF analysis between two cultural groups is provided by Oishi (2007), who compared Chinese and American responses on various items, rated using five response categories from 1 = not at all to 5 = extremely.

The results are depicted by plotting average responses for each group on two axes. The x-axis indicates respondents' latent scores, in z score intervals of 1, 2, and 3 SDs above and below the mean on each item. The y-axis indicates the average probability of actually endorsing a particular response category for each item. The results are shown by two Item Characteristic Curves (ICC), one for each cultural group. The invariance of these ICCs can then be compared. For example, if one ICC shows, that for scale item 1, Chinese rating the item as 1 SD below the mean are most likely to endorse response category 2 (a little), while Americans rating the item 1 SD below their mean are most likely to endorse response category 4 (quite a bit), then the two groups are clearly responding to the item in different ways. A formal test, to determine the significance of this difference, has been described by Reise et al. (1993) in the form of the G^2 index.

6.2.2   Factorial Invariance

The second method, to be described in detail here, is Multi-Group Confirmatory Factor Analysis. Like IRT, factorial invariance requires that the association between the scale items and the latent factors of individuals does not depend on group membership. Factorial invariance also requires that the latent factor scores, the expected values, the co-variances between items, and the unexplained variance unrelated to the latent factors are also equal across the comparison groups.

Measurement invariance is perhaps the most important statistical technique providing insights into the reasons for observed SWB differences between demographic groups, especially between different cultural groups. As judged by the authoritative Van De Schoot et al. (2015, p. 1), 'when a strict form of measurement invariance is not established, and one must conclude that respondents attach different meanings to survey items, this makes it impossible to make valid comparisons between latent factor means … or regression coefficients'. As Vandenberg and Lance (2000, p. 55) correctly conclude, 'generally, comparisons on non-equivalent measures should not be undertaken'.

Testing for measurement invariance involves simultaneous multi-group confirmatory factor analysis, described by Chen et al. (2005), with technical reviews of the procedure available from Brown (2015), Gregorich (2006), and Vandenberg and Lance (2000). Overviews of invariance applications in cross-cultural studies appear in Davidov et al. (2014) and Millsap (2012).

6.2.3   Levels of Factorial Invariance

Four incremental levels of measurement invariance can be tested as follows:

1. Configural (equal form; dimensional). The number of factors and the pattern of factor-indicator relations are identical (invariant) across groups. In this case, factor loadings, intercepts, and residual variances are freely estimated (Horn et al., 1983); that is, these statistics are not required to be identical between groups.

Three additional forms of factorial invariance were first described by (Meredith, 1993). These involve the progressive constraint of elements in the factorial matrices, to invariance, across groups. Meeting these constraints allows ever stronger statements about cross-group differences on measured and latent variables.

2. Metric (weak factorial invariance; equal loadings; pattern). The factor loading of each item on the latent factor is invariant across groups (factor pattern coefficients are invariant across groups). This requires that the unit and the interval of the latent factor are equal across groups (Chen, 2007).

3. Scalar (strong factorial invariance; equal intercepts). Assuming metric invariance, scalar additionally requires that regressions of items onto their associated common factors yields a vector of intercept terms that is invariant across groups. Thus, when observed scores are regressed on each factor, the item intercepts are equal across groups.

4. Strict (strict factorial; equal residual variances). 'The additional constraints that define the strict factorial invariance model involve the unique factor invariances, or measurement residuals' (Widaman & Reise, 1997, p. 295). The residual is the difference between the observed mean value of an item and the *estimated* value of that item. In addition to the equality of factor loadings and intercepts, strict invariance requires that the residual variances of the observed item scores, which are not accounted for by the factors, are equal across groups.

Each of these four conditions corresponds to a multiple-group confirmatory factor model with specific constraints. The tenability of each model is tested using a likelihood ratio test or other indices of fit. Meaningful comparisons between groups usually require that all four conditions are met, which is strict invariance. However, among scales in general, strict measurement invariance is rarely achieved (Stevelink & van Brakel, 2013; Van De Schoot et al., 2015). This raises the question of what kinds of between-group comparisons can be made with a scale that fulfils each level of measurement invariance.

6.3   Comparing Invariant Groups

6.3.1   Defensible Group Comparisons

Different kinds of statistical comparisons are valid at each level of measurement invariance. These are as follows:

Configural

None (Gregorich, 2006; Widaman & Reise, 1997). That is, even though the confirmatory factor analysis has confirmed that the number of factors and the pattern of factor–indicator relationships are invariant between groups, this does not allow the observed differences between groups to be regarded as valid.

If the scale(s) do(es) not factor as intended, the analysis can be repeated omitting items which are causing the factorial failure. However, when this is done, the new analysis is being performed on a scale that has not been confirmed, and the factor analysis is exploratory (Byrne, 2010).

Metric

Metric invariance allows the comparison of factor variances and structural relations (e.g. correlations between variables) across groups (Asparouhov & Muthén, 2014; Gregorich, 2006). Achieving metric invariance means that the factor loading of each item on the latent factor is the same across groups. Thus, the unit and the interval of the latent factor are equal across groups (Chen, 2007). Once metric invariance has been demonstrated, scalar invariance may be tested to examine whether the intercept of each item is the same across groups, in addition to the equality of factor loadings.

Scalar and Strict

The reason these two categories of invariance are being considered together is that many researchers and statisticians are conflicted as to the advice that should be given. On the one hand, there is no doubt that the valid comparison of *latent* mean scores requires strict invariance (Meredith, 1993). Other authors agree that failure to achieve strict invariance means 'one must conclude that respondents attach different meanings to survey items, this makes it impossible to make valid comparisons between *latent* factor means' (Van De Schoot et al., 2015, p. 1).

Many other authors agree, therefore, that in the absence of strict invariance, comparisons between *observed* mean scores are invalid in terms of the assumption of latent construct equivalence (e.g. Jang et al., 2017). This is a serious conclusion in cross-cultural research, where the meaning that respondents give to scale items is at the heart of understanding why empirical comparisons of subjective wellbeing differ between national groups. Only with strict invariance can the mean scores of the invariant items be considered to represent equivalent latent constructs between groups.

On the other hand is the practical reality that very few scales demonstrate strict invariance. This is most especially so when the comparative groups are culturally different (Stevelink & van Brakel, 2013; Van De Schoot et al., 2015). In their 26-country comparison of the Satisfaction with Life Scale, Jang et al. (2017, p. 566) state that 'strict invariance was not tested because this approach is too stringent and unrealistic (citing Byrne, 1994)'.

This acceptance, that demonstrating strict invariance in cross-cultural comparisons is just too hard has led to widespread, if grudging, advice that scalar invariance is sufficient grounds to validly compare group mean scores. 'If strong factorial invariance holds, group differences in both means and variances on the latent variables, which represent the constructs in psychological theories, are reflected in group differences in means and variances on the measured variables . . . additional constraints . . . resulting in strict factorial invariance, are nice but not necessary' (Widaman & Reise, 1997, pp. 295–296). Other authors agree (e.g. Jang et al., 2017; Meredith, 1993)

While this 'practical' solution to the difficulty of demonstrating strict invariance is convenient for researchers, it also introduces an obscurantist element into cross-cultural comparisons of subjective wellbeing. It does not allow the valid interpretation of cross-cultural mean score differences which, surely, is the whole point of demonstrating invariance. Take for example the commonly reported finding that the SWB levels of Chinese samples are lower than Australian samples (Chen & Davey, 2008). The usual interpretation is that the 'life quality' in China is lower than it is in Australia. However, such an interpretation rests, fundamentally, on the assumption that respondents from both cultures are responding to the scale items in the same way. Unless this can be established, interpretation in terms of differential life quality cannot be verified.

So, the temptation in such circumstances is to perform group-mean comparisons using scalar or partial scalar invariance, even knowing that such results serve to perpetuate misconceptions regarding the interpretation of cultural group differences. The correct interpretation of such results is stated by Żemojtel-Piotrowska et al. (2017) – that scalar invariance allows a valid comparison of the correlates of the factor scores across countries, but not a comparison of the raw (observed) scores.

In summary, the power of measurement invariance for cross-cultural research is that the technique allows researchers to make an assumption that the latent construct being measured is validly represented by the observed mean scores. In other words, strict invariance has demonstrated response equivalence in latent factors between cultural groups. If these criteria are not met, various rescue strategies are available. I will now discuss these in the context of cross-cultural research.

6.3.2 Strategic Follow-Up to Failed Invariance

Invariance testing simply achieves a reasonable level of assurance that the observed factor mean scores represent equivalent latent factors. However, as discussed by Widaman and Reise (1997), invariance testing does not indicate *why* differences in factor structure occur, but simply *where* they occur in the factor structure. The 'why' differences (causes) of non-invariance might lie within any psychological, cultural, or economic conditions which are contributing to the observed group differences. Yet understanding why some items are non-invariant is the key to understanding cross-cultural comparisons. So, in the face of failed invariance, additional investigations are warranted.

There are various available follow-up procedures, all of which involve identifying non-invariant items. At a high level of statistical sophistication, DeRoover et al. (2014) suggest a method of identification based on cluster-wise simultaneous component analysis. An alternative strategy is offered by Barendse et al. (2014), who use a Bayesian restricted (latent) factor analysis. Several comments derive from this.

1. These sophisticated techniques are important tools in the quest to unravel the cause of each invariance. However, there will be occasions in which no amount of further analysis will achieve strict invariance. When this occurs, researchers should be forthright in stating that the scale cannot be validly used for comparative purposes. An exemplary lead has been supplied by Lommen et al. (2014) in their study of post-traumatic stress. After failing to achieve strict invariance, they concluded that their measured pre- and post-symptom scores represented separate constructs.
2. Following failed invariance, the most commonly used strategy is to test for partial invariance. This technique was first described by Byrne et al. (1989). To demonstrate partial factorial invariance, only some of the factor loadings (Metric) or vector of intercept terms (Scalar) are constrained to invariance across groups, and the remaining estimates may vary freely across groups.
3. After demonstrating partial invariance, authors generally take their analyses no further. However, a more informative process, most especially if partial-strict invariance has been found, is to run the analysis again after having deleted data from the non-invariant items.

6.4   *Creating Invariant Scale Short Forms*

The technique of deleting non-invariant items following demonstration of partial invariance is methodologically acceptable (Chen et al.,

2005; Gregorich, 2006). It results in an explicit description of the structure of a successful short form of the scale. The additional computation of means, variances, and correlations provided by the short form, when compared to those provided by the full scale, informs an understanding of the psychometric character of the abbreviated scale. Such results also provide a comparison for future researchers.

However, two concerns attend the use of this procedure. The first is that the scale, as published, is different from the short form that has been used to make the between-group comparisons. This difference could have serious implications for interpreting the results because it may be measuring a different construct from the original scale. So whether this invariant latent factor is func-tionally the same or different from that derived from the original scale needs to be established.

A second concern is that the number of items representing the latent factor has been reduced. This focuses attention on the minimum number of items required to support a reliable invariant scale. Gregorich (2006) makes the statistical case that only one or two items are theoretically sufficient for this purpose, and Jang et al. (2017), in their comparison of 26 countries using the SWLS, use just two items. However, if comparative scale variance is of interest, then three items are the minimum number required to support an invariant factor.

These caveats aside, the power of invariance testing, coupled with a reduction in the number of scale items to the invariant minimum, has the potential to revolutionize cross-cultural research. Two examples of this reduction will now be considered, both involving the simplest, single-factor scales used to measure SWB. Because each of these scales has already been described in detail, only the results of invariance testing will be presented.

6.4.1   Satisfaction with Life Scale

Each of the following studies, used for this description of invar-iance, has compared different cultural groups. Because the inten-tion is simply to indicate how a reduced number of items can create greater likelihood of invariance, the details of these studies have been minimized, and the concentration is on identifying the most robust items, as follows:

Jang et al. (2017) compared 26 countries. They found partial scalar for items 1 and 3 only.

Wu et al. (2009) test-retested Taiwanese college students. At two months they found partial strict for items 1, 2, 4, 5, and at six months partial scalar for items 2, 3, 4.

Zanon et al. (2014) compared Brazil and the United States. They found invariance for items 1, 2, 3.

From this simple comparison, the number of items involved in the invariance sub-scales is as follows:

Item (number of times invariant): 1 (2); 2 (2); 3 (3); 4 (1); 5 (1). From this it might be concluded that a short-form of the SWLS involving only items 1, 2, and 3 can be tentatively recommended for cross-cultural research.

As further evidence for this selection, Jang et al. (2017) demonstrated that dissimilar mean age across countries significantly affected the intercept of Item 4, 'So far I have gotten the important things I want in life', which is endorsed more by older than by younger respondents. In addition, using Item Response Theory, Oishi (2010) described his (Oishi, 2006) study on American and Chinese college students. Based on the strict criteria, only item 2 showed non–Differential Item Functioning (DIF). Item 4 had the largest DIF. Items 4 and 5 showed an item bias across the two cultural groups.

In summary, there is a preliminary body of evidence suggesting that the SWLS can be improved by creating a short form from items 1, 2, and 3.

6.4.2 Personal Wellbeing Index

The PWI comes in three versions: for adults, children, and people with an intellectual or cognitive disability. The descriptions to follow are restricted to the adult version of the scale.

When the seven PWI domains are regressed against GLS, the design intention is that each domain will make a unique variance contribution to GLS. However, as described in the previous Basic Measures section, this does not generally occur. While the three 'golden' domains of living standard, relationships, and achieving in life do make a predictable unique contribution in Australia, in other countries this predictability is greatly weakened.

These results, from use of multiple regression, seem to give some hint that the validity of the PWI could be improved by a reduction to just three items. The key test of this possibility is through invariance testing. However, supporting evidence in relation to the other four domains is mixed:

Health: Among elderly Spanish adults, Forjaz et al. (2012) found health and standard not to fit a Rasch (IRT) model. In Australia also, health does not usually make a unique variance contribution to GLS. The relevance of health to SWB may depend, at least in part, on the availability of health care. In Spain and Australia, the populations are well covered by a system of universal health care. In countries where this does not apply, the health domain may have more relevance to SWB.

Community: Żemojtel-Piotrowska et al. (2017) tested invariance among college students in 26 countries. They only achieved partial scalar. The two non-invariant items are achieving in life and community. The problems with community are evident even in Australian data, where the domain has a very uncertain relationship with GLS (International Wellbeing Group, 2013). The additional problems with translation have been noted previously, and confirmed by Møller et al. (2015), who reported a qualitative study which explored the meaning of the isiXhosa version of the PWI. They found the items personal relationships and community connectedness as having nearly identical meaning. In summary, this appears to be a poorly performing domain.

Safety: Misajon et al. (2016) compared adults living in Australia or Canada using Rasch analysis. The only very mild disordered thresholds were for safety. In support, the multiple regression analyses against GLS using Australian data usually show no unique variance to be contributed by safety. Other countries also tend to show this same result, with a few exceptions (International Wellbeing Group, 2013). This is also a poorly performing domain.

Future security: This domain performs poorly in Australia. Internationally, it does not always translate easily. It can be confused with safety, and is sometimes interpreted as 'financial security'.

In summary, there appears to be weak evidence that the creation of a three-item short form of the PWI may improve the scale's performance in terms of between-group comparisons. If this were so, then it would comprise the three 'golden' domains of standard, relationships, and achieving.

The reason for the pre-eminence of these three domains is that each encompasses a double benefit: they provide both resources to avoid homeostatic defeat and resources to recover when things go wrong. Money does it through the purchase of both protective and recovery resources. Relationships do this through social support (protective) and intimate sharing (recovery). Meaningful activity does it through providing a sense of purpose and structure to life (protective) while also facilitating connection to similarly oriented people, and if the activity is a paid job, then it also provides income (recovery).

In summary, both the Personal Wellbeing Index and the Satisfaction with Life Scale seem amenable to strict invariance when some items are deleted. For each scale, a three-item short form might then allow valid cross-cultural comparisons of observed scale mean scores. This possibility, however, remains to be verified through further empirical testing.

6.4.3   Conclusion on Invariance

The most obvious conclusion from the information presented here is that, even using the simplest scales that appear to be short, single-factor measures of SWB, it has not been possible to achieve strict invariance between cross-cultural groups in the examples given. Clearly, therefore, seeking invariance of more complex multi-item scales would almost certainly be futile. It must also be concluded that, in their published form, it is likely that no published multi-item SWB scales are valid when used for cross-cultural comparisons.

To recap the story so far, the first three steps of invariance testing concern the interaction of the items with one another within the factor-analytic frame. These steps check that when the scale items are responded to by people from each group, their data yield the same number of factors (configural), the same factor loadings (metric), and the same intercepts (scalar). The final step of strict invariance is different from this. The criterion for strict invariance concerns the variance remaining after accounting for the variance explained by the first three steps. Strict invariance requires that this residual variance is equal between the groups.

If this unequal residual variance is caused by some systematic difference between cultural groups, then it can be predicted that strict invariance will be impossible to achieve; the residuals must always be different between groups differing in culture. However, if such a source of residual variance could be identified and measured, then the source of residual variance could be accounted for. This would achieve two outcomes. First, it would go a long way to understanding why the residuals are preventing strict invariance. Second, it would allow an understanding that the differences between the groups' observed mean scores are accounted for by the identified source. A potential source of such difference between cultural groups is cultural response bias.

6.5   Invariance and Cultural Response Bias

As I have discussed, it is common to find published lists comparing countries on their levels of subjective wellbeing or mood happiness (e.g. Deaton, 2008; Helliwell et al., 2017; OECD, 2017a). The authors inevitably find that the level of SWB within Confucianism-influenced societies (mainland China, Taiwan, Korea, Japan, Vietnam, and Singapore) is lower than in Australia and North America. The usual interpretation of the discrepancy, either implicitly or explicitly, is that it represents valid international differences in subjective life quality.

Making such a conclusion ignores the influence of cultural differences in the ways people process information and respond to evaluative personal questions. Both children and adults are chronically exposed to systematic ways of thinking and behaving, which are key to distinguishing their culture from another (see e.g. Steel et al., 2017). Of special relevance to the current discussion are the culture-specific response styles when answering personal questions.

Demonstrated variations in response styles have a long history, going back at least 70 years to Cronbach (1946). Even at that time he noted 'numerous studies' showing that scores on standardized test instruments may be influenced by variables other than the one supposedly tested. For example, the typical test used to measure the level of skills and knowledge for schoolchildren, at that time, asked them to rate a statement as either true of false. The assumption is that both types of response are equally valid indicators of the student's ability. However, Cronbach notes this is not so. When the scores from each child were calculated, based on whether each statement was correctly marked 'true' or 'false', 'the correlation of the two performance scores is near zero even when the test as a whole is reliable' (p. 475).

Cronbach attributed this difference to various levels of an 'acquiescent' response style, defined as 'any tendency causing a person consistently to give different responses to test items than he would when the same content is presented in a different form' (p. 476). That is, when in doubt, students with an acquiescent response style are more likely to respond 'true' rather than 'false'. The result is that their scores on true statements are higher than their scores on false statements.

In summary, items requiring a 'true' response are not psychometrically equivalent on the trait being measured to items requiring a 'false' response (see also Cronbach, 1941, 1942). Cronbach referred to this tendency as a 'response set' and considered the tendency to acquiesce to be a stable individual difference – in other words, attributable to personality. Additionally, the probability of acquiescent behaviour can be enhanced by cultural training.

6.5.1   The Influence of Culture

In the micro-environment of institutional living, people with an intellectual disability learn that an acquiescent response style is adaptive for their survival. Such people, with low levels of understanding of and control over their living environment, learn social response strategies that include an overly developed inclination to agree positively when asked a question by a member of the institutional staff (Sigelman et al., 1981).

Similar response biases can be shown to develop within minority groups living in the broader society. The first such demonstration was by Bachman and O'Malley (1984), who reported differing levels of acquiescent response style between Black and White Americans. The authors are coy about speculating as to the cause of these differences. However, in the 1980s, Black Americans were a severely disadvantaged minority group. They comprised about 12% of the population, with a median household income of approximately half that of White Americans (DeNavas-Walt et al., 2012). Adopting an acquiescent response style was adaptive when interacting with White Americans.

In addition to learning such simple defensive rules, societies also teach other systematic response biases through the relative structure of language, which influences people's world view (see Kay & Kempton, 1984). In addition, personal interactions within each culture teach the rules and expectations of their society. It is therefore quite logical that different cultural experiences likely differentially influence the way people respond to personal questions (Kirmayer, 1989). Of special relevance to SWB research is the extent to which people from different cultures are willing to express high levels of personally felt positivity on a self-rating scale of happiness or satisfaction.

Response biases at the level of culture imply that everyone raised in that culture has, to some extent, acquired a response tendency that is systematically different from people in a different culture. The evidence supporting the likely existence of cultural response biases is now overwhelming, with many reviews describing such apparent tendencies (e.g. Chen & Davey, 2008; Oishi, 2010). Such evidence, if valid, clearly implies that simple interpretation of SWB difference between countries cannot be taken at face value. However, additional information regarding the potential cause and influential extent of such bias is required before it can be considered a reliable influence on SWB data.

While much relevant information is available to be used as evidence, the data are drawn from comparisons involving a large number of countries. This is a problem because the direction of response biases, in relation to a standard American comparison, is often uncertain. Thus, in order to simplify further discussion, the results to be reviewed are confined to comparisons of populations influenced by Confucian belief, as listed earlier, with those of Western populations (e.g. Chen & Davey, 2008). Within this frame of comparison, it is proposed that people raised in Confucianism-influenced societies tend to hold back from regis-tering extreme scores. In contrast, people raised in Western socie-ties are more likely to simply report how they feel, using the whole extent of the response scale options.

In seeking a description of the nature of cultural training which could induce the Confucian response bias, the study by Lau et al. (2005) involving Hong Kong Chinese has already been described. In addition and in confirmation of their findings, the accounts by Iwata and colleagues (Iwata et al., 1994; Iwata et al., 1995), in Japan, are enlightening. They suggested that the Japanese have a 'tendency to suppress positive affect expression'. They proposed that while the expression of positive feelings about oneself are normally part of American culture (Ying, 1989), in traditional Japanese and Chinese Confucian society individual psychological wellbeing is subordinated to the wellbeing of the group (Ying, 1988). Thus, the maintenance of social harmony is a most impor-tant value, and people have learned since childhood to understate their own virtues and not to behave assertively. This may lead them to pay more attention to group situations and interpersonal relations than do Americans. This tendency is reflected in a more relativistic or external standard for their expression of feelings about themselves, causing them to judge positive affect through a comparison with others, as a relativistic and modest judgement.

Indeed, the virtue of modesty is a traditional norm induced by Confucian ethics. Even when people feel very good, they may hesitate to voice this opinion because such behaviour is impolite. The result of this training is that, on a printed questionnaire, Japanese and Chinese respondents are more likely to rate themselves as having a moderate rather than a high level of positive affect. This accounts for why they evidence a preference for mid-scale responses to positively worded, but not to negatively worded, questions of personal feelings.

6.5.2   Response Bias and Negative Wording

Perhaps the most convincing evidence that cultural response biases exist is that such biases are far more likely to be demonstrated in positive appraisals than in negative ones. To give some examples, Iwata et al. (1995) compared self-ratings from Japan and the United States. Whereas the self-ratings on negatively worded items were comparable, on the positive items Japanese respondents scored lower. Similarly, Lee et al. (2002) compared Chinese, Japanese, and Americans responses to self-ratings on positively or negatively worded statements. They found that, for positively worded statements, both Chinese and Japanese were more likely than Americans to choose a response from the middle of the Likert scale. However, the three groups showed the same response pattern for negatively worded items.

In one contrary study, Kim et al. (2008) found that, as expected, American undergraduates scored higher than Chinese undergraduates on the Rosenberg Self Esteem Scale (Rosenberg, 1979). However, when the five positively worded and five negatively worded items were rephrased to be all positive, the groups did not differ. On the other hand, when the items were all reworded to be negative, the American self-esteem was higher. However, this result may not be reliable. Not only are the reported significance levels weak, but the interpretation of the result is complex. Both cultural groups increased their self-esteem scores when the items were all positively worded, and decreased their scores when the items were negatively worded. In other words, both cultural groups responded in the same direction to the rewording. The significant difference came about because, when using the negative version, the Chinese dropped more than the Americans. So their result should be worded: 'Chinese self-esteem is reduced more than American self-esteem by using negatively worded items.' This result needs replication.

Overall, there is reasonably strong evidence that the Confucian vs. American cultural response bias is confined to positively worded self-appraisals.

6.5.3 Response Bias and Demographic Advantage

Countries differ in both wealth and culture. Since SWB is sensitive to both types of influence, it has been commonly assumed that the lower levels of SWB within Confucianism-influenced countries, compared with Western countries, have been due to lower income. A more informed view is that such differences can be accounted for by a combination of income and cultural response bias.

Evidence in support of this view is supplied by Lau et al. (2005). They report that both average income and SWB were lower in Hong Kong than in Australia. However, the authors argue that the lower SWB can be attributed to culture as well as to differential income. They reason:

(a) Because people in Hong Kong will be avoiding the ends of the response scale, the cultural response bias will tend to truncate the distribution of SWB, making it more leptokurtic or peaked. The result will be a smaller standard deviation and a reduced mean score, because the strongest effect of the bias will be to reduce the frequency of responding at the top of the distribution.

(b) Because more people in Hong Kong will be in economic distress, this will tend to extend the SWB distribution downwards, making the distribution more negatively skewed and platykurtic or flat. This will tend to decrease the mean and raise the standard deviation.

In summary of these two influences, the mean level of SWB should be less in Hong Kong due to the combined influences of the response bias and income inequality. The standard deviation, on the other hand, should remain much the same due to the opposing forces described. This prediction was confirmed. The mean SWB was higher for the Australian sample and there was no difference in the standard deviation of the two samples. The authors concluded that this is evidence of a cultural response bias, because the effects of the income inequality alone would act to both reduce the mean and extend the standard deviation.

There is also other evidence showing that the Confucian–Western SWB difference is not due simply to disadvantaged demographics. For example, there are cross-cultural studies demonstrating SWB differences between samples matched on age, gender, and education (Iwata et al., 1994; Iwata et al., 1995), while others have used age and education as covariates (Lee et al., 2002).

In summary, it seems reasonable to propose that the Confucian–Western SWB difference is not simply due to differences in income, education, gender, or age.

6.5.4 Response Bias and Question Type

It is possible that there is a particular form of scale construction that engenders the reduced Confucian response. However, the evidence against this proposition is substantial.

In addition to the SWLS and PWI, cultural response bias has been found using a wide variety of scales. For example, Iwata and colleagues (Iwata et al., 1994; Iwata et al., 1995) used the Center for Epidemiologic Studies Depression Scale (Radloff, 1977), an instrument with a sub-scale of four positively worded items (feeling good, hopeful, happy, enjoyed) lying among 16 negatively worded items.

At a more conceptually complex level, Lee et al. (2002) found cultural response bias using Antonovsky's Sense of Coherence scale (Antonovsky, 1987) 13-item short form (Ryland & Greenfield, 1991) with simplified format devised by Nyamathi (1993). This scale is interesting in the present context because its aim is not to measure wellbeing in the sense of happiness or satisfaction, but rather to reflect the 'salutogenic' approach to adaptive coping. As described by Antonovsky (1993), the scale 'does not refer to a specific type of coping strategy, but to factors which, in all cultures, always are the basis for successful coping with stressors' (p. 726). Each scale item is a different statement, and many of these statements contain two parts. For example, 'Many people, even those with a strong character-sometimes feel like sad sacks (losers) in certain situations. How often have you felt this way in the past?' The statements are rated according to various anchors, such as, for example, 'never' to 'very often' or 'you over-estimated or under-estimated its importance' to 'you saw things in the right proportion'. Thus, the overall impression of the scale is one of complexity and not likely to support a simple response set. Yet the authors reported cultural response bias.

A further possibility is that questions tapping individualism induce lower ratings within Confucian societies. Evidence against this is supplied by Chen et al. (1995), who used a questionnaire covering a broad range of topics concerning ideas, values, attitudes, beliefs, and self-evaluations related to school and daily life. Four items tapped an orientation towards individualism or collectivism. Individualism was stronger in the United States than in Japan or Taiwan. This was accompanied by more frequent use of extreme values and less frequent use of the midpoint. However, the difference in individualism could not account for the large differences found in the comparisons of country-level means.

In summary, it can be concluded that evidence for the existence of the Confucian response bias has been reported in data gained from a wide variety of positive items, embedded within a variety of scales. Moreover, evidence of the bias remains after accounting for income, education, and age differences. All of this evidence, however, is circumstantial. No study has yet directly measured cultural response bias, and until such evidence is forthcoming, researchers will tend to persist with simplistic interpretations of between-country differences in subjective wellbeing. Perhaps the judicious use of measurement invariance can identify response bias as responsible for a portion of SWB differences between cultural groups.

7 Investigating Response Bias and Invariance

The earlier section on measurement invariance has concluded that empirical comparisons between groups, using observed data from scales, can only be validly attributed to the dependent variable (SWB) if the groups show strict factorial invariance. In the case of cross-cultural groups, however, this introduces a conundrum. If, as suggested by Jang et al. (2017), cultural response bias is the source of the residual variance, and therefore the reason for non-invariance, then the country mean scores cannot be used to demonstrate cultural response bias because the comparative measures are not invariant.

There may be a way of resolving this problem. It requires a consideration of the sources of variance that influence group differences in SWB when cultures are being compared, with a view to determining the relative influence of cultural response bias. The design of such a study requires careful planning in all aspects of data collection, to the point that it will look more like a laboratory study than a survey. The intention is to create the most favourable circumstances possible to test whether cultural response bias can be demonstrated with as little equivocation as possible.

7.1 A Potential Study

The spirit of this hypothetical study is to make all aspects of the methodology as simple, reliable, and controlled as possible. I suggest that the design of such a study would incorporate the following features:

1. The choice of cultures. No more than two cultures should be compared. This makes the logistic requirements of the study simpler to manage and the interpretation of the results more direct. The two cultures must have a well-documented, potential differential response bias, such as Australia and Japan.

2. The choice of samples. It is essential that the samples to be compared are as homogeneous as possible. The intention of the study is only to determine the existence of cultural response bias. If this is successful, then subsequent studies can answer questions of generalization to whole national populations. In this spirit, the samples should be equivalent in the following respects:

   2.1 The availability of objective homeostatic resources. The major ones are money (a determined range around the national median income), being in a relationship, and being employed.

   2.2 Level of education. It is crucial for the testing of invariance that all respondents find the scale items easily understood. This could be achieved by setting a minimal education level, such as completion of high school.

   2.3 Age: Population levels of SWB change with age, showing a dip around 40–50 years. It is also important to investigate the strongest possible influence of culture, so respondents should be aged from 50 to 60 years.

   2.4 Level of acculturation. All respondents must be fully and currently immersed in their own cultural group. This eliminates international students, expatriates, and people who have spent significant time studying or working overseas, especially if this took place in the opposite culture.

3. Instrumentation. The scales of measurement must comprise only the simplest items, and fewest in number, necessary to reliably measure the SWB construct and to calculate variance.

These items must be core to all human thinking about self, and represent unambiguously high relevance for representing the SWB construct. It is recommended to use a shortened version of either the SWLS or the PWI. While the more precise content of these scales remains to be finalized, from the evidence presented in this review, the best bet for the SWLS are items 1, 2, and 3. The items for the PWI are standard, relationships, and achieving.

4. Data collection. Data must be collected under determined supervision. This means by face-to-face interview, written questionnaire, telephone, or electronic device. However, data are potentially biased or unreliable if they are collected by unsupervised students, recruited by commercial agencies from their maintained 'panels', or recruited from advertising on social media (Weinberg et al., under review).

5. Data processing.

   5.1 Psychopathology: Unpredictable error variance is generated by the inclusion of respondents who have a level of SWB <50 points (Richardson et al., 2016). Such respondents should be deleted from the sample prior to analysis.

   5.2 Data cleaning. Data need to be inspected for outliers. A table showing all means, standard deviations, and correlations can be inspected for anomalies.

7.1.1 Interpretation of Results

If these methodological recommendations are followed, then there are four outcome possibilities from a test of invariance between two cultures:

(a) Strict invariance is achieved and there *is no* difference in the level of observed factor mean scores for SWB between the groups. **Interpretation:** The previously reported group differences have been either an artifact of an imposed etic set of items and/or caused by between-group inequality of homeostatic resources.

(b) Strict invariance is achieved and there *is a* difference in SWB between the groups. **Interpretation:** Since the uncontrolled, systematic difference between the two groups, is cultural response bias, and because the members of each culture have perceived and responded to all of the scale items in the same way, it can likely be concluded that the group differences approximate the power of cultural response bias to change reported levels of SWB.

(c) Scalar but not strict invariance is achieved, and there *is no* difference in SWB between the groups. **Interpretation:** Because so many prior studies have demonstrated a difference in SWB at the level of scalar invariance, this result may indicate something untoward with the samples. In any event, the two factor mean scores cannot be validly compared, since members of each culture have not perceived and responded to all of the scale items in the same way. Each cultural group has effectively responded to a different scale.

(d) Scalar but not strict invariance is achieved, and there *is a* difference in SWB between the groups. **Interpretation:** The result cannot be unambiguously interpreted due to the presence of unexplained residual variance. However, both the failure to achieve strict invariance and the different levels of SWB could be attributable to cultural response bias. Additionally, since controls 1–2 and 2–2 have been imposed, the most likely cause of the difference is cultural response bias.

In conclusion, even if a single well-controlled study could show, without reasonable doubt, the existence and strength of cultural response bias, this will have a major impact on the understanding, and especially the interpretation, of comparative SWB data from different cultural groups. It will allow a quite different appraisal to be made of cross-cultural comparisons, and allow such information to be subsequently elaborated into a valid picture of SWB levels between nations.

8 Summary and Conclusions

In order to make a comprehensive assessment of life quality, it is necessary to employ both objective and subjective indicators. The level and distribution of key objective indicators, such as income, intimate partnership, and active occupation, are useful guides to population resilience, as measured by the level of subjective well-being (SWB). The SWB level reflects the extent to which the population is effectively utilizing such resources to manage their wellbeing and, in particular, the proportion of the population suffering homeostatic failure (a level <50 points) and risk of depression.

In order to understand the interaction between these objective and subjective social indicators, the variables must be reliably and validly measured. This is a relatively simple task in relation to the objective indicators. They are represented by tangible variables, whose measurement can be verified by a number of people. The measurement of SWB is far more difficult. It requires agreement among researchers as to the scale used to make the measurement, as well as the conditions under which the measurement takes place. Additionally, because the accuracy of the reported data can only be verified by the person providing the data, the scientific verification of measurement validity and reliability becomes dependent on the application of complex statistics.

Notwithstanding these difficulties, great strides of understanding have been made over the past 50 years of systematic research in this area. It is now understood that a few scales of measurement provide much the same data, allowing conceptual cohesion of the SWB construct. It is also understood that SWB is normally stable, held close to each person's set-point by a system of homeostasis. And further, that significant movements of SWB away from set-point represent the influence of emotions as they briefly overwhelm the capacity of homeostasis to maintain stability. These understandings make SWB a very useful indicator of normal psychological functioning at both the level of the individual and the level of populations.

The usefulness of SWB as a subjective social indicator is, however, restricted to its application within individual cultures. This usefulness does not apply to comparative SWB between countries. The reason, I propose, is differences in culture which influence the way people respond to questions yielding SWB data. Because culture trains people how to interact with others, inter alia it trains people how to appropriately respond to questions concerning their personal feelings. As a consequence, people from different cultures are likely to respond differently to standard questions designed to measure SWB. If such cultural response bias can be confirmed, the direct comparison of observed inter-nation levels of SWB is likely to be invalid as an indicator of relative differences in subjective life quality.

One of the keys to advancing understanding of response bias is to have instruments which validly measure SWB between different cultural groups. The construction of such instruments can be informed by the application of measurement invariance, and that has been a major focus of this review. Although the discussion has demonstrated that none of the instruments investigated can yield valid comparative data, there are signs that modifications could improve their performance in this regard.

The two instruments investigated in this review are the simplest multi-item scales available. Both the Satisfaction with Life Scale and the Personal Wellbeing Index each comprise five to seven items which form a single factor. Moreover, the output of both instruments share about half of their variance, both with one another and with General Life Satisfaction, showing they substantially measure the same construct. However, neither instrument is able to meet the criterion of strict invariance. Unequal residual variance at this analytic step represents unexplained variance, which has the potential to cause the latent factor means and the observed means to be different. One interpretation of the cause of this failure of strict invariance is that the respondents from different cultures are responding to the scale items in different ways.

It is proposed here that, in order to facilitate the interpretation of invariance testing, as many as possible of the potential sources of residual variance should be eliminated. This can be achieved by applying systematic procedures to the data collection methodology. One is to ensure, as far as possible, that the samples from each culture are comparable in terms of objective homeostatic resources (especially income, intimate partnerships, and active occupation) and demographic profiles (especially age). All of these are known to influence homeostatic resilience, so this procedure simply ensures that the residual variance is not caused by inequality in these variables.

The second procedure is to strip each of the measurement instruments down to its bare essentials. This means selecting the three items from the scale which most closely meet the requirement for strict invariance. Three items is the minimum allowing variance calculations. This reduction also has the advantage of comprising only the best-suited items for the task in each application. The inclusion of items beyond this minimum simply adds to the probability that culture-specific items will add error variance.

The third procedure is to ensure that pathological data are removed prior to analysis. These are defined as data from people in homeostatic defeat, identified by PWI scores of <50 points. Richardson et al. (2016) demonstrated that such data yield an abnormal factor structure characterized by higher variability and weak domain inter-correlations. An alternative procedure, to achieve a similar end, has been described by Misajon et al. (2016), who eliminated data from respondents who scored <70 points on a question of general health.

I have discussed potential outcomes from the hypothetical study. At best, they provide a clear demonstration of the extent to which cultural response bias can influence the comparative level of SWB. Other outcomes allow for less certain conclusions, or even a conclusion that the bias cannot be detected using the prescribed methodology. However, no matter the outcome, this discussion leads to an inescapable realization: Valid cross-cultural comparisons of SWB require far higher attention to methodological detail than they have received to date.

In drawing this discussion to a close, there is no doubt that the creation of a valid cross-cultural measure of SWB is a worthy goal.

When countries are compared on their levels of SWB, more than national pride is at stake. These comparative data are fundamental to understanding how major homeostatic resources interact with cultural differences to support normal levels of wellbeing. This understanding can only be validly achieved when the role of cultural response bias is understood.

Acknowledgements

I thank Matthew Fuller-Tyszkiewicz for his suggestions regarding the statistical descriptions. This work was supported by the Ministry of Education of the Republic of Korea and the National Research Foundation of Korea (NRF-2016S1A3A2924563).

References

Ager, A. (2002). 'Quality of life' assessment in critical context. *Journal of Applied Research in Intellectual Disabilities, 15*, 369–376.

Alvarez, I., Bados, A., & Pero, M. (2010). Factorial structure and validity of the multicultural Quality of Life Index. *Quality of Life Research, 19*, 225–229.

Andrews, F. M., & Withey, S. B. (1976). *Social indicators of well-being: Americans' perceptions of life quality*, New York: Plenum Press.

Anglim, J., Weinberg, M. K., & Cummins, R. A. (2015). Bayesian hierarchical modeling of the temporal dynamics of subjective well-being: A 10 year longitudinal analysis. *Journal of Research in Personality, 59*, 1–14.

Antonovsky, A. (1987). *Unraveling the mystery of health: How people manage stress and stay well*. San Francisco: Jossey-Bass.

Antonovsky, A. (1993). The structure and properties of the sense of coherence scale. *Social Science & Medicine, 36*, 725–733.

Aranda, M., & Knight, B. (1997). The influence of ethnicity on the caregiver stress and coping process: A sociocultural review and analysis. *The Gerontologist, 37*, 342–354.

Asparouhov, T., & Muthén, B. (2014). Multiple-group factor analysis alignment. *Structural Equation Modeling: A Multidisciplinary Journal, 21*, 495–508.

Australian Centre on Quality of Life (ACQOL). (2017). *Australian Centre on Quality of Life – Directory of Instruments*. Available at: http://www.acqol.com.au/instruments#measures

Bachman, J. G., & O'Malley, P. M. (1984). Yea-saying, nay-saying, and going to extremes: Black-white differences in response styles. *Public Opinion Quarterly, 48*, 491–509.

Barendse, M. T., Albers, C., Oort, F., et al. (2014). Measurement bias detection through Bayesian factor analysis. *Frontiers in Psychology, 5*, 1087.

Batinic, B., Selenko, E., Stiglbauer, B., et al. (2010). Are workers in high-status jobs healthier than others? Assessing Jahoda's latent benefits of employment in two working populations. *Work & Stress, 24*, 73–87.

Bauer, R. A. (1966) *Social indicators*. Cambridge, MA: MIT Press.

Bedin, L. M., & Sarriera, J. C. (2015). A comparative study of the subjective well-being of parents and adolescents considering gender, age and social class. *Social Indicators Research, 120,* 79–95.

Bentham, J. (1780). *An introduction to the principles of morals and legislation*. London: T. Payne.

Bentham, J. (1789). *An introduction to the principles of morals and legislation*. Garden City, NY: Doubleday.

Berger, S. L., Kouzarides, T., Shiekhattar, R., et al. (2009). An operational definition of epigenetics. *Genes & Development, 23,* 781–783.

Bieda, A., Hirschfeld, G., Schönfeld, P., et al. (2017). Universal happiness? Cross-cultural measurement invariance of scales assessing positive mental health. *Psychological Assessment, 29,* 408–421.

Bloom, A. (1981). *The linguistic shaping of thought*, Hillsdale, NJ: Erlbaum.

Blore, J. D., Stokes, M. A., Mellor, D., et al. (2011). Comparing multiple discrepancies theory to affective models of subjective wellbeing. *Social Indicators Research, 100,* 1–16.

Braungart, J. M., Plomin, R., DeFries, J. C., et al. (1992). Genetic influence on tester-rated infant temperament as assessed by Bayley's infant behavior record: Nonadoptive and adoptive siblings and twins. *Developmental Psychology, 28,* 40–47.

Brickman, P., Coates, D., & Janoff-Bulman, R. (1978). Lottery winners and accident victims: Is happiness relative? *Journal of Personality and Social Psychology, 36,* 917–927.

Brown, T. (2015). *Confirmatory factor analysis for applied research* (2nd ed.). New York: Guilford Press.

Bunnin, N., & Yu, J. (2008). *The Blackwell dictionary of Western philosophy*. Malden, MA: Wiley.

Burns, J. H. (2005). Happiness and utility: Jeremy Bentham's equation. *Utilitas, 17,* 46–61.

Buss, D. M., & Greiling, H. (1999). Adaptive individual differences. *Journal of Personality, 67,* 209–243.

Byrne, B. M. (1994). Testing for the factorial validity, replication, and invariance of a measuring instrument: A paradigmatic application based on the Maslach Burnout Inventory. *Multivariate Behavioral Research, 29,* 289–311.

Byrne, B. M. (2010). *Structural equation modelling in AMOS: Basic concepts, applications, and programming* (2nd ed.). New York: Routledge.

Byrne, B. M., Shavelson, R. J., & Muthén, B. (1989). Testing for the equivalence of factor covariance and mean structures: The issue of partial measurement invariance. *Psychological Bulletin, 105,* 456–466.

Campbell, A., Converse, P. E., & Rodgers, W. L. (1976). *The quality of American life: Perceptions, evaluations, and satisfactions.* New York: Russell Sage Foundation.

Cannon, W. B. (1932). *The wisdom of the body.* New York: Norton.

Capic, T., Li, N., & Cummins, R. A. (2018). Confirmation of subjective wellbeing set-points: Foundational for subjective social indicators. *Social Indicators Research. 137* (1), 1–28. doi:10.1007/s11205-017-1585-5.

Casas, F. (2016). Children, adolescents and quality of life: The social sciences perspective over two decades. In F. Maggino (Ed.), *A life devoted to quality of life – Festschrift in honor of Alex C. Michalos* (pp. 3–21). Dordrecht, Netherlands: Springer.

Casas, F., González, M., Figuer, C., et al. (2009). Satisfaction with spirituality, satisfaction with religion and personal well-being among Spanish adolescents and young university students. *Applied Research in Quality of Life, 4,* 23–45.

Cella, D. F., Tulsky, D. S., Gray, G., et al. (1993). The Functional Assessment of Cancer Therapy scale: Development and validation of the general measure. *Journal of Clinical Oncology, 11,* 570–579.

Chang, H. H., & Nayga, R. M. (2010). Childhood obesity and unhappiness: The influence of soft drinks and fast food consumption. *Journal of Happiness Studies, 11,* 261–276.

Chen, C., Lee, S.-Y., & Stevenson, H. W. (1995). Response style and cross-cultural comparisons of rating scales among East Asian and North American students. *Psychological Science, 6,* 170–175.

Chen, F. F. (2007). Sensitivity of goodness of fit indexes to lack of measurement invariance. *Structural Equation Modeling, 14,* 464–504.

Chen, F. F., Sousa, K. H., & West, S. G. (2005). Teacher's corner: Testing measurement invariance of second-order factor models. *Structural Equation Modeling, 12,* 471–492.

Chen, Z., & Davey, G. (2008). Normative life satisfaction in Chinese societies. *Social Indicators Research, 89,* 557–564.

Clark, A. E, Diener, E., Georgellis, Y., et al. (2008). Lags and leads in life satisfaction: A test of the baseline hypothesis. *Economic Journal, 118,* F222–F243.

Clarke, P. J., Marshall, V. W., Ryff, C. D., et al. (2001). Measuring psychological well-being in the Canadian Study of Health and Aging. *International Psychogeriatrics, 33,* 79–90.

Cronbach, L. J. (1941). An experimental comparison of the multiple true-false and multiple multiple-choice tests. *Journal of Educational Psychology, 32,* 533–543.

Cronbach, L. J. (1942). Studies of acquiescence as a factor in the true-false test. *Journal of Educational Psychology, 33,* 401–415.

Cronbach, L. J. (1946). Response sets and test validity. *Educational and Psychological Measurement, 6,* 475–494.

Cummins, R. A. (1997). Self-rated quality of life scales for people with an intellectual disability: A review. *Journal of Applied Research in Intellectual Disability, 10,* 199–216.

Cummins, R. A. (1998). The second approximation to an international standard of life satisfaction. *Social Indicators Research, 43,* 307–334.

Cummins, R. A. (2000). Personal income and subjective well-being: A review. *Journal of Happiness Studies, 1,* 133–158.

Cummins,R. A. and H. Nistico (2002). "Maintaining life satisfaction: The role of positive cognitive bias." Journal of Happiness Studies 3(1): 37-69.

Cummins, R. A., Walter, J., & Woerner, J. (2007). Australian Unity Wellbeing Index: Report 16.1 - "The Wellbeing of Australians - Groups with the highest and lowest wellbeing in Australia", Australian Centre on Quality of Life, School of Psychology, Deakin University, Melbourne. http://www.acqol.com.au/projects#reports

Cummins, R. A. (2010). Fluency disorders and life quality: Subjective wellbeing vs. health related quality of life. Invited paper. *Journal of Fluency Disorders, 35,* 161–172.

Cummins, R. A., Woerner, J., Weinberg, M., et al. (2013c). Australian Unity Wellbeing Index: -Report 30.0 - The Wellbeing of Australians: Social media, personal achievement, and work. Melbourne, Australian Centre on Quality of Life, School of Psychology, Deakin University. http://www.acqol.com.au/projects#reports.

Cummins, R. A., et al. (2014a). "A demonstration of set-points for subjective wellbeing." Journal of Happiness Studies 15: 183-206.

Cummins, R. A. (2014). Subjective indicators of wellbeing. In A. Michalos (Ed.), *Encyclopedia of quality of life and well-being research* (pp. 6429-6431). Dordrecht, Netherlands: Springer.

Cummins, R. A. (2016). The theory of subjective wellbeing homeostasis: A contribution to understanding life quality. In F. Maggino (Ed.), *A life devoted to quality of life – Festschrift in honor of Alex C. Michalos* (pp. 61–79). Dordrecht, Netherlands: Springer.

Cummins, R. A., Eckersley, R., Pallant, J., et al. (2003). Developing a national index of subjective wellbeing: The Australian Unity Wellbeing Index. *Social Indicators Research, 64*, 159–190.

Cummins, R. A., & Gullone, E. (2000). Why we should not use 5-point Likert scales: The case for subjective quality of life measurement. *Second International Conference on Quality of Life* in Cities, Singapore: National University of Singapore.

Cummins, R. A., Woerner, J., Weinberg, M., et al. (2012). *Australian Unity Wellbeing Index: – Report 28.0 – The Wellbeing of Australians – The impact of marriage.* Available at: http://www.acqol.com.au/projects#reports

Davern, M., Cummins, R. A., & Stokes, M. (2007). Subjective wellbeing as an affective/cognitive construct. *Journal of Happiness Studies, 8*, 429–449.

Davidov, E., Meuleman, B., Cieciuch, J., et al. (2014). Measurement equivalence in cross-national research. *Annual review of sociology, 40*, 55–75.

Deaton, A. (2008). Income, health, and well-being around the world: Evidence from the Gallup World Poll. *Journal of Economic Perspectives, 22*, 53–72.

Deci, E. L., & Ryan, R. M. (2008b). Hedonia, eudaimonia, and well-being: An introduction. *Journal or Happiness Studies, 9*, 1–11.

DeNavas-Walt, C., Proctor, B. D., & Smith, J. C. (2012). *U.S. Census Bureau, current population reports, P60-243, income, poverty, and health insurance coverage in the United States: 2011.* Washington, DC: U.S. Government Printing Office.

DeRoover, K., Timmerman, M. E., De Leersnyder, J., et al. (2014). What's hampering measurement invariance: Detecting non-invariant items using clusterwise simultaneous component analysis. *Frontiers in Psychology, 5*, 604. doi: 10.3389/fpsyg.2014.00604

deSilva, M. J., Huttly, S. R., Harpham, T., et al. (2007). Social capital and mental health: A comparative analysis of four low income countries. *Social Science & Medicine, 64*, 5–20.

deSilva, M. J., McKenzie, K., Huttly, S. R., et al. (2005). Social capital and mental illness: A systematic review. *Journal of Epidemiology and Community Health, 59*, 619–627.

Diener, E. (1984). Subjective well-being. *Psychological Bulletin, 95*, 542–575.

Diener, E. (2006). Guidelines for national indicators of subjective well-being and ill-being. *Journal of Happiness Studies, 7*, 397–404.

Diener, E., Emmons, R. A., Larsen, R. J., et al. (1985). The satisfaction with life scale. *Journal of Personality Assessment, 49*, 71–75.

Diener, E., Scollon, C. N., & Lucas, R. E. (2004). The evolving concept of subjective well-being. The multifaceted nature of happiness. In P. T. Costa & I. C. Siegler (Eds.), *Recent advances in psychology and aging* (pp. 188–219). Amsterdam: Elsevier Science BV.

Dixon, P. N., Bobo, M., & Stevick, R. A. (1984). Response differences and preferences for all-category-defined and end-defined Likert formats. *Educational and Psychological Measurement, 44*, 61–66.

Drasgow, F. (1987). Study of the measurement bias of two standardized psychological tests. *Journal of Applied Psychology, 72*, 19–29.

Drasgow, F., & Kanfer, R. (1985). Equivalence of psychological measurement in heterogeneous populations. *Journal of Applied Psychology, 70*, 662–680.

Ensel, W. M., Lin, N. (1991). The life stress paradigm and psychological distress. *Journal of Health and Social Behavior, 32*, 321–341.

Forjaz, M. J., Ayala, A., Rodriguez-Blazquez, C., et al. (2012) Rasch analysis of the international wellbeing index in older adults. *International Psychogeriatrics, 24*, 324–332.

Freyd, M. (1923). The graphic rating scale. *Journal of Educational Psychology, 14*, 83–102.

Fromm, E. (1947). *Man for himself: An inquiry into the psychology of ethics.* New York: Holt, Rinehart & Winston.

Goldberg, D. P., & Williams, P. A. (1988). *User's guide to the general health questionnaire.* Windsor, UK: NFER/Nelson.

Gregorich, S. E. (2006). Do self-report instruments allow meaningful comparisons across diverse population groups? Testing measurement invariance using the confirmatory factor analysis framework. *Medical Care, 44*, S78–S94.

Gross, B. M. (1966b). The state of the nation: Social systems accounting. In R. A. Bauer (Ed.), *Social Indicators* (pp. 154–271). Cambridge, MA: MIT Press.

Gurin, G., Veroff, J., & Feld, S. (1960). *Americans view their mental health: A nationwide interview survey.* New York: Basic Books.

Hammond, T., Weinberg, M. K., & Cummins, R. A. (2014). The dyadic interaction of relationships and disability type on informal carer subjective well-being. *Quality of Life Research, 23*, 1535–1542.

74 References

Hartmann, G. W. (1934) Personality traits associated with variations in happiness. *Journal of Abnormal and Social Psychology, 29*, 202–212.

Helliwell, J. F., Layard, R., & Sachs, J. (2017). *World happiness report 2017.* New York: Sustainable Development Solutions Network.

Henderson, S. (1977). The social network, support and neurosis. The function of attachment in adult life. *British Journal of Psychiatry, 131*, 185–191.

Hildingh, C., & Baigi, A. (2010). The association among hypertension and reduced psychological well-being, anxiety and sleep disturbances: A population study. *Scandinavian Journal of Caring Sciences, 24*, 366–371.

Hofstede, G. (1984). *Culture's consequences: International differences in work-related values.* Beverley Hills, CA: Sage.

Holton, S., Fisher, J., & Rowe, H. (2010). Motherhood: Is it good for women's mental health? *Journal of Reproductive and Infant Psychology, 28*, 223–239.

Horn, J. L., McArdle, J. J., & Mason, R. (1983). When is invariance not invarient: A practical scientist's look at the ethereal concept of factor invariance. *Southern Psychologist, 1*, 179–188.

Human Development Index. (2007/2008). *Fighting climate change: Human solidarity in a divided world.* New York: United Nations Development Program & Palgrave Macmillan.

Human Development Index. (2017). Geneva, Switzerland: United Nations Development Program, http://hdr.undp.org/en/content/human-development-index-hdi.

Huntington, S. (1996). *The clash of civilizations and remaking of world order.* New York: Touchstone.

Inglehart, R. (1997). *World values surveys; GNP/capita purchasing power estimates from World Bank, World Development Report 1977.* Washington, DC: World Bank. Available at: http://margaux.grandvinum.se/SebTest/wvs/articles/folder published/articlebase56.

International Wellbeing Group. (2013). *Personal wellbeing index manual* (5th ed.). Available at: http://www.acqol.com.au/instruments# measures

Iwata, N., Roberts, C. R., & Kawakami, N. (1995). Japan-US comparison of responses to depression scale items among adult workers. *Psychiatry Research, 58*, 237–245.

Iwata, N., Saito, K., & Roberts, R. E. (1994). Responses to a self-administered depression scale among younger adolescents in Japan. *Psychiatry Research, 53*, 275–287.

Jang, S., Kim, E. S., Cao, C., et al. (2017). Measurement invariance of the Satisfaction With Life Scale across 26 countries. *Journal of Cross-Cultural Psychology, 48*, 560–576.

Jones, L. V., & Thurstone, L. L. (1955). The psychophysics of semantics: An experimental investigation. *The Journal of Applied Psychology, 39*, 31–36.

Joshanloo, M. (2013). A comparison of Western and Islamic conceptions of happiness. *Journal of Happiness Studies, 14*, 1857–1874.

Kafka, G. J., & Kozma, A. (2002). The construct validity of Ryff's Scales of Psychological Well-Being (SPWB) and their relationship to measures of subjective well-being. *Social Indicators Research, 57*, 171–190.

Kanai, R., & Rees, G. (2011). The structural basis of inter-individual differences in human behaviour and cognition. *Nature Reviews Neuroscience, 12*, 231–242.

Kay, P., & Kempton, W. (1984). What is the Sapir-Whorf hypothesis? *American Anthropologist, 86*, 65–79.

Kim, Y. H., Peng, S. Q., & Chiu, C. Y. (2008). Explaining self-esteem differences between Chinese and North Americans: Dialectical self (vs. self-consistency) or lack of positive self-regard. *Self and Identity, 7*, 113–128.

Kirmayer, L. J. (1989). Cultural variations in the response to psychiatric disorders and emotional distress. *Social Science & Medicine, 29*, 327–339.

Land, K. C., & Michalos, A. C. (2018). Fifty years after the social indicators movement: Has the promise been fulfilled? An Assessment and an Agenda for the Future. *Social Indicators Research 135*(3), 835–868.

Lau, A. L. D., Cummins, R. A., & McPherson, W. (2005). An investigation into the cross-cultural equivalence of the Personal Wellbeing Index. *Social Indicators Research, 72*, 403–430.

Lavric, M., & Flere, S. (2008). The role of culture in the relationship between religiosity and psychological well-being. *Journal of Religion & Health, 47*, 164–175.

Lee, J. W., Jones, P. S., Mineyama, Y., et al. (2002). Cultural differences in responses to a Likert scale. *Research in Nursing and Health, 25*, 295–306.

Leung, S. O. (2011). A comparison of psychometric properties and normality in 4-5-6 and 11 point Likert scales. *Journal of Social Service Research, 37*, 412–421.

Likert, R. (1932). A technique for the measurement of attitudes. *Archives in Psychology, 140,* 1–55.

Lommen, M. J. J., Van De Schoot, R., & Engelhard, I. M. (2014). The experience of traumatic events disrupts the measurement invariance of a posttraumatic stress scale. *Frontiers in Psychology, 5,* 1304–1313.

Longo, Y. (2015). The simple structure of positive affect. *Social Indicators Research, 124,* 183–198.

Lowenthal, M. F., & Haven, C. (1968). Interaction and adaptation: Intimacy as a critical variable. *American Sociological Review, 33,* 20–30.

Lykken, D. T., & Tellegen, A. (1996). Happiness is a stochastic phenomenon. *Psychological Science, 7,* 186–189.

Magana, S., & Smith, M. J. (2006). Psychological distress and well-being of Latina and non-Latina White mothers of youth and adults with an autism spectrum disorder: Cultural attitudes towards coresidence status. *American Journal of Orthopsychiatry, 76,* 346–357.

Magilvy, J., Congdon, J., Martinez, R., et al. (2000). Caring for our own: Health care experiences of rural Hispanic elders. *Journal of Aging Studies, 14,* 171–191.

Marin, G., & Marin, B. (1991). *Research with Hispanic populations.* Newbury Park, CA: Sage.

Matell, M. S., & Jacoby J. (1972). Is there an optimal number of alternatives for Likert-scale items? Effects of testing time and scale properties. *Journal of Applied Psychology, 56,* 506–517.

McEwen, B. S., & Wingfield, J. C. (2003). The concept of allostasis in biology and biomedicine. *Hormones and Behavior, 43,* 2–15.

McGill, V. J. (1968). *The idea of happiness.* New York: Frederick A. Praeger.

McGue, M., Bacon, S., & Lykken, D. T. (1993). Personality stability and change in early adulthood: A behavioral genetic analysis. *Developmental Psychology, 29,* 96–109.

McHorney, C. A., Ware, J. E., & Raczek, A. E. (1993). The MOS 36-item short-form health survey (SF-36): II. Psychometric and clinical tests of validity in measuring physical and mental health constructs. *Medical Care, 31,* 247–263.

Mellenbergh, G. J. (1989). Item bias and item response theory. *International Journal of Educational Research, 13,* 127–143.

Meredith, W. (1993). Measurement invariance, factor analysis and factorial invariance. *Psychometrika, 58,* 525–543.

Merriam-Webster. (2018). *Online dictionary*. Available at: http://www .merriam-webster.com.

Miller, G. A. (1956). The magical number seven, plus or minus two: Some limits on our capacity for processing information. *Psychological Review, 63*, 81–97.

Millsap, R. E. (2012). *Statistical approaches to measurement invariance*, New York: Routledge.

Misajon, R., Pallant, J., & Bliuc, A-M. (2016). Rasch analysis of the Personal Wellbeing Index. *Quality of Life Research, 25*, 2565–2569.

Moksnes, U. K., Løhre, A., Byrne, D. G., et al. (2014). Satisfaction with life scale in adolescents: Evaluation of factor structure and gender invariance in a Norwegian sample. *Social Indicators Research, 118*, 657–671.

Møller, V., Roberts, B., & Zani, D. (2015). The Personal Wellbeing Index in the South African IsiXhosa Translation: A qualitative focus group study. *Social Indicators Research, 124*, 835–862.

National Institutes of Health. (2017) *Roadmap Epigenomics Project.* Washington, DC: NIH. Available at: http://www.roadmapepigenomics .org/overview.

Nyamathi, A. M. (1993). Sense of coherence in minority women at risk for HIV infection. *Public Health Nursing, 10*, 151–158.

Oatley, K., & Johnson-Laird, P. N. (1987). Towards a cognitive theory of emotions. *Cognition and Emotion, 1*, 29–50.

OECD. (2017a). *PISA 2015 Results (Volume III): Students' Well-Being, PISA*, Paris: OECD Publishing.

OECD. (2017b). *Better Life Index (life satisfaction)*, Paris: OECD. Available at: http://www.oecdbetterlifeindex.org/topics/life-satisfaction/.

Oishi, S. (2006). The concept of life satisfaction across cultures: An IRT analysis. *Journal of Research in Personality, 40*, 411–423.

Oishi, S. (2007). The application of structural equation modeling and item response theory to cross-cultural positive psychology research. In A. D. Ong & M. H. M. Van Dulmen (Eds.), *Handbook of methods in positive psychology* (pp. 126–138). New York: Oxford University Press.

Oishi, S. (2010). Culture and well-being: Conceptual and methodological issues. In E. Diener, J. F. Helliwell, & D. Kahneman (Eds.), *International differences in well-being* (pp. 34–69). Oxford: Oxford University Press.

Olsson, C. A., McGee, R., Nada-Raja, S., et al. (2013). A 32-year longitudinal study of child and adolescent pathways to well-being in adulthood. *Journal of Happiness Studies, 14*, 1069–1083.

Pavot, W., & Diener, E. (1993). Review of the satisfaction with life scale. *Psychological Assessment, 5,* 164–172.

Radloff, L. S. (1977). The CES-D scale: A self-report depression scale for research in the general population. *Applied Psychological Measurement, 1,* 385–401.

Reise, S. P., Widaman, K. F., & Pugh, R. H. (1993). Confirmatory factor analysis and item response theory: Two approaches for exploring measurement invariance. *Psychological Bulletin, 114,* 552–566.

Renn, D., Pfaffenberger, N., Platter, M., et al. (2009). International Well-Being Index: The Austrian version. *Social Indicators Research, 90,* 243–256.

Richardson, B., Fuller-Tyszkiewicz, M. D., Tomyn, A. J., et al. (2016). The psychometric equivalence of the Personal Wellbeing Index for normally functioning and homeostatically defeated Australian adults. *Journal of Happiness Studies, 17,* 627–641.

Rosenberg, M. (1979). *Conceiving the self.* New York: Basic Books.

Rothbaum, F., Weisz, J. R., & Snyder, S. S. (1982). Changing the world and changing the self: A two-process model of perceived control. *Journal of Personality and Social Psychology, 42,* 5–37.

Røysamb, E., Nes, R. B., & Vittersø, J. (2014). Well-being: Heritable and changeable. In K. M. Sheldon & R. E. Lucas (Eds.), *Stability of happiness: Theories and evidence on whether happiness can change* (pp. 9–36). Philadelphia: Elsevier.

Russell, J. A. (1980). A circumplex model of affect. *Journal of Personality and Social Psychology, 39,* 1161–1178.

Russell, J. A. (2003). Core affect and the psychological construction of emotion. *Psychological Review, 110,* 145–172.

Ryan, R. M., & Deci, E. L. (2001). On happiness and human potentials: A review of research on hedonic and eudaimonic well-being. *Annual Review of Psychology, 52,* 141–166.

Ryff, C. D. (1989). Happiness is everything, or is it? Explorations on the meaning of psychological well-being. *Journal of Personality and Social Psychology, 57,* 1069–1081.

Ryland, E., & Greenfield, S. (1991). Work stress and well being: An investigation of Antonovsky's sense of coherence model. *Journal of Social Behavior and Personality, 6,* 39–54.

Sabogal, F., Marin, G., Otero-Sabogal, R., et al. (1987). Hispanic familism and acculturation: What changes and what doesn't. *Hispanic Journal of Behavioral Science, 9,* 397–412.

Sarason, B. R., Sarason, I. G., & Pierce, G. R. (1990b). *Social support: An interactional view*, New York: John Wiley & Sons.

Sarason, S. B. (1977). *The psychological sense of community: Prospects for a community psychology*. London: Jossey-Bass.

Schulz R., & Heckhausen J. (1996) A life span model of successful aging. *American Psychologist, 51*, 702–714.

Seidlitz, L., & Diener, E. (1993). Memory for positive versus negative life events: Theories for the differences between happy and unhappy persons. *Journal of Personality and Social Psychology, 64*, 654–664.

Shurgot, G., & Knight, B. (2004) Preliminary study investigating acculturation, cultural values, and psychological distress in Latino caregivers of dementia patients. *Journal of Mental Health and Aging, 10*, 183–194.

Sigelman, C. K., Budd, E. C., Spanhel, C. L., et al. (1981). When in doubt, say yes: Acquiescence in interviews with mentally retarded persons. *Mental Retardation, 19*, 53–58.

Silva, A. D., do Céu Taveira, M., Marques, C., et al. (2015). Satisfaction with Life Scale among adolescents and young adults in Portugal: Extending evidence of construct validity. *Social Indicators Research, 120*, 309–318.

Smith, A. (1776). *An inquiry into the nature and caufes of the wealth of nations*, London: W. Strahan and T. Cadell. Available at: http://books.google.bg/books?id=C5dNAAAAcAAJ&pg=PP7#v=onepage&q&f=true (accessed January 13, 2018).

Smith, A. (1869). *An inquiry into the nature and causes of the wealth of nations*, Oxford: Clarendon Press. Available at: https://books.googleusercontent.com/books/content?

Steel, P., Taras, V., Uggerslev, K., et al. (2017). The happy culture: A theoretical, meta-analytic, and empirical review of the relationship between culture and wealth and subjective well-being. *Personality and Social Psychology Review*, before print, 1–42. doi:10.1177/1088868317721372

Stening, B. W., & Everett, J. E. (1984). Response styles in a cross-cultural managerial study. *Journal of Social Psychology, 122*, 151–156.

Stevelink, S. A. M., & van Brakel, W. H. (2013). The cross-cultural equivalence of participation instruments: A systematic review. *Disability and Rehabilitation, 35*, 1256–1268.

Tavor, I., Jones, O. P., Mars, R., et al. (2016). Task-free MRI predicts individual differences in brain activity during task performance. *Science, 352*, 216–220.

Tellegen, A., Lykken, D. T., Bouchard, T. J. J., et al. (1988). Personality similarity in twins reared apart and together. *Journal of Personality and Social Psychology, 54*, 1031–1039.

Thompson. R. F. (2009). Habituation: A history. *Neurobiology of Learning and Memory, 92*, 127–134.

Tiliouine, H., Cummins, R. A., & Davern, M. (2006). Measuring wellbeing in developing countries: The case of Algeria. *Social Indicators Research, 75*, 1–30.

Tomyn, A. J., & Cummins, R, A. (2011). Subjective wellbeing and home-ostatically protected mood: Theory validation with adolescents. *Journal of Happiness Studies, 12*, 897–914.

Trewin, D. (2001). *Frameworks for Australian social statistics.* Canberra: Australian Bureau of Statistics. Available at: http://www.ausstats.abs .gov.au/ausstats/free.nsf/0/D609B8E54F0EDCA8CA256AE30004282D/ $File/41600_2001.pdf.

van Beuningen, J. (2012). *The satisfaction with life scale examining construct validity.* Discussion paper (2012209). The Hague: Statistics Netherlands.

van Beuningen, J., & de Jonge, T. (2011). *The PWI Index – Construct validity for the Netherlands.* Discussion paper (201124). The Hague: Statistics Netherlands.

Van De Schoot, R., Schmidt, P., De Beuckelaer, A., et al. (2015). Editorial: Measurement invariance. *Frontiers in Psychology, 6*, 1–4.

Vandenberg, R. J., & Lance, C. E. (2000). A review and synthesis of the measurement invariance literature: Suggestions, practices, and recommendations for organizational research. *Organizational Research Methods, 3*, 4–70.

Veenhoven, R. (1996). Developments in satisfaction-research. *Social Indicators Research, 37*, 1–46.

Veenhoven, R. (2010). Greater happiness for a greater number: Is that possible and desirable? *Journal of Happiness Studies, 11*, 605–629.

Veenhoven, R. (2017). World database of happiness. (accessed November 4, 2017).

Watson, G. B. (1930). Happiness among adult students of education. *Journal of Educational Psychology, 21*, 79–109.

Weinberg, M. K., Webb, D. A., Gwozdz, W., et al. (under review) Subjective wellbeing and recruitment from incentivised online panels: Caveat emptor. *Journal of Wellbeing Assessment.*

Wessman, A. E., & Ricks, D. F. (1966). *Mood and personality.* New York: Holt, Rinehart & Winston.

WHOQOL Group. (1994). Development of the WHOQOL: Rationale and current status. *International Journal of Mental Health, 23*, 24–56.

Widaman, K. F., & Reise, S. P. (1997). Exploring the measurement invariance of psychological instruments: Applications in the substance use domain. In K. J. Bryant, M. Windle, & S. G. West (Eds.), *The science of prevention: Methodological advances from alcohol and substance abuse research* (pp. 281–324). Washington, DC: American Psychological Association.

World Bank (1997). "World Values Surveys; GNP/Capita purchasing Power Estimates from World Bank, World Development Report 1977, Inglehart, R." Collection of Graphs Presenting WVS Data.

Wu, C. H., Chen, L. H., & Tsai, Y.-M. (2009). Longitudinal invariance analysis of the satisfaction with life scale. *Personality and Individual Differences, 46*, 396–401.

Wyatt, R. C., & Meyers, L. S. (1987). Psychometric properties of four 5-point Likert type response scales. *Educational and Psychological Measurement, 47*, 27–35.

Ying Y.-W. (1989). Nonresponse on the center for epidemiological studies-depression scale in Chinese Americans. *International Journal of Social Psychiatry, 35*, 156–163.

Ying, Y. -W. (1988). Depressive symptomatology among Chinese-Americans as measured by the CES-D. *Journal of Clinical Psychology, 44*, 739–746.

Zanon, C., Bardagi, M. P., Layous, K., et al. (2014). Validation of the satisfaction with life scale to Brazilians: Evidences of measurement noninvariance across Brazil and US. *Social Indicators Research, 119*, 443–453.

Żemojtel-Piotrowska, M., Piotrowski, J. P., Cieciuch, J., et al. (2017). Measurement invariance of Personal Well-Being Index (PWI-8) across 26 countries. *Journal of Happiness Studies, 18*, 1697–1711.

Cambridge Elements ☰

Psychology and Culture

Kenneth D. Keith
University of San Diego

Kenneth D. Keith is author or editor of more than 160 publications on cross-cultural psychology, quality of life, intellectual disability, and the teaching of psychology. He was the 2017 president of the Society for the Teaching of Psychology.

About the series
Elements of Psychology and Culture will feature authoritative surveys and updates on key topics in cultural, cross-cultural, and indigenous psychology. Authors are internationally recognized scholars whose work is at the forefront of their subdisciplines within the realm of psychology and culture.

Cambridge Elements ☰
Psychology and Culture

Elements in the series

Printed in the United States
By Bookmasters